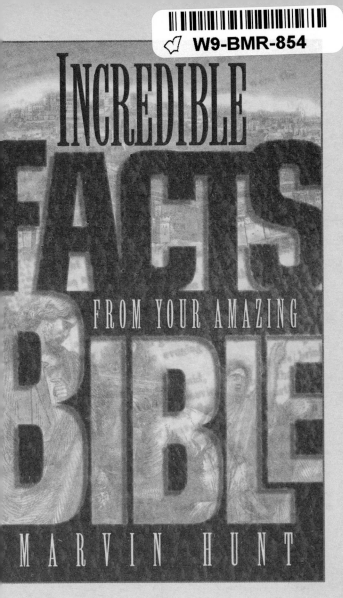

INCREDIBLE FACTS

FROM YOUR AMAZING

BIBLE

MARVIN HUNT

REVIEW AND HERALD® PUBLISHING ASSOCIATION
HAGERSTOWN, MD 21740

The author assumes full responsibility for the accuracy of all
facts and quotations as cited in this book.

Texts credited to NIV are from the *Holy Bible, New International Version.* Copyright © 1973, 1978, 1984, International Bible
Society. Used by permission of Zondervan Bible Publishers.
Bible texts credited to TEV are from the *Good News
Bible*—Old Testament: Copyright © American Bible Society
1976; New Testament: Copyright © American Bible Society
1966, 1971, 1976.

This book was
Edited by Gerald Wheeler
Cover designed by Willie Duke
Typeset: 11.5/13 Cochin

PRINTED IN U.S.A.

00 99 98 97 96   10 9 8 7 6 5 4 3 2 1

R&H Cataloging Service
Hunt, Marvin F., 1941-
    Incredible facts from your amazing Bible.

    1. Bible—Miscellanea.   I. Title.

                    220

ISBN 0-8280-1103-6

Acknowledgments

A heartfelt thank-you
for all those who helped me
write this book.
They include
Frank Holbrook, biblical accuracy;
Noble B. Vining, technical accuracy;
Jennifer Rash, readability;
and Judy (Juderific) Hunt
for always supporting me
and providing tea at 3:00.

Contents

The Mystery of What Jesus Really Looked Like/7

Just How Far Is It From Jerusalem to . . ./11

Surprising Facts About Angels
That Few People Know!/13

Secret Books of the Bible?/15

Is Jesus Mentioned Outside the Bible?/17

The Bible and Supernatural Guidance/20

Why We Can Trust the Accuracy of the Bible/22

Amazing Statistics/25

The Mysterious Books Rejected by All Faiths/28

Why and How to Study the Bible/30

How Did the Bible Get Its Name?/33

The Name They Would Not Say/34

Will I Know You in Heaven?/35

The Bible and the Seven-Day Week/36

How Did They Decide Which Books
to Include in the Bible?/41

The Difficulty of Bible Translation/44

What About All of Those Bible Translations?/46

The Church the Bible Founded/50

The Mystery Surrounding Jesus' Real Birthday/60

The Bible and the Mystery of Death/62

Paul and the Slave/64

Unusual Things in the Bible/67

Why Many Bible Words Are in Italics/71

Why People Are Baptized
at the Leaning Tower of Pisa/73

Don't Confuse Us With Them/75

The Mystery Revealed of How to Live Forever/77

The Mystery of the Number 666/80

Can Bible Numbers Be Dangerous?/82

To Eat . . . or Not to Eat?/86

Why Jesus Went to Church on Saturday/87

The Bible and the Mystery of God's Day/89

The Mystery of the Unpardonable Sin/99

Hotter Than Hell?/101

In What Unusual Places
Did Early Christians Worship?/103

The Mystery of the Mark of the Beast/105

Fascinating Facts About Easter Sunday/108

Facts You Need to Know About Bible Study Tools/109

Does It Really Say That in the Bible?/112

Little-known Facts About
How Ancient Writings Were Made/113

What Does the Bible Really Say About Heaven?/115

What Was That in Roman Time?/119

The Mystery of the Lost Books of the Bible/121

Where 43 of the Bible's Most Interesting
Things Are Found/123

What the Bible Has Meant in My Life: A Personal Note/125

The Mystery of
What Jesus Really Looked Like

Jesus, born of a Jewish mother and raised in the Jewish culture of the time, must have resembled the other people of the times. Not one of His disciples or other followers ever described His personal appearance or mentioned anything that would have set Him apart physically from everyone else. Any picture or likeness of Him that we have today is purely imaginary. However, we do have one debated reference in Isaiah 53 that deserves consideration. Many feel that Isaiah 53:2 gives a physical description of Jesus as the suffering Messiah to come. It reads: "He had no beauty or majesty to attract us to him, nothing in his appearance that we should desire him" (NIV).

Scholars argue whether the chapter is a prophecy regarding the coming Messiah or a prophecy of the terrible suffering the Jews would undergo in their future. Whatever conclusion you come to, it does seem logical that Jesus' appearance would intentionally be one that did not attract people because of any physical attributes. Probably Jesus was not seven feet tall and the most handsome man in all of Palestine. Such an idea would be contrary to a principle God laid down in 1 Samuel 16:7 when He explained how He chose David to be king: "For the Lord seeth not as man seeth; for man looketh on the outward appearance, but the

Lord looketh on the heart." If Jesus had any special attractiveness, it would be that of His character and spiritual presence.

Many Jews and early Christians assumed that the Old Testament prohibited images, thus restricting the making of either pictures or statues. However, the Old Testament did not oppose art. God commanded Moses to make a serpent of brass, and Solomon's Temple had all kinds of beautiful artwork decorating it.

Probably because of the early Christians' misunderstanding of image making, we find few specific depictions of Christ prior to the time of Emperor Constantine (died A.D. 337). Instead, Christians symbolically portrayed Jesus as a shepherd, a lamb, a fisherman, or most often with the symbol of a fish. The earliest known picture of Christ occurs in the catacombs as part of a scene portraying the resurrection of Lazarus. Dated to the middle of the second century, it shows Jesus in a Roman tunic, beardless, and with short hair and large eyes. The picture's location is an area called the Cappella Greca (Greek Chapel).

The earliest known Christian house church, at Dura Europus on the upper Euphrates, contains a painting of Jesus dating to about A.D. 240. It depicts Christ as a beardless young man dressed in a tunic.

A description of the physical appearance of Christ appears in an apocryphal letter of Publius Lentullus, "president of the people of

Jerusalem [no such office existed]," who supposedly wrote a letter to the Roman senate discussing Jesus. Though the letter is not authentic and can be traced no earlier than the fourth century, it strongly influenced later portrayals of Christ. The letter says: "His hair is of the color of wine, and golden at the root; straight, and without lustre, but from the level of the ears curling and glossy, and divided down the centre after the fashion of the Nazarenes. His eyes are blue, and extremely brilliant . . ."

Please note the reference to "after the fashion of the Nazarenes." Scholars conclude that it should read "Nazarites." By definition, a Nazarite was a Jewish person who took strict religious vows, such as neither to cut his hair nor to drink wine.

John the Baptist was a Nazarite. This meant that he was specially dedicated to God and would abstain from all grape products, leave his hair uncut, and refrain from approaching any dead body (see Num. 6:2-5). Jesus grew up in a small town called Nazareth. Inhabitants of Nazareth were referred to negatively as being Nazarenes. Jesus was a Nazarene, but not a Nazarite. Some commentators have mistakenly said Jesus was a Nazarite, but in Luke 7:34 we read otherwise: "The Son of man [Jesus here refers to Himself] is come eating and drinking; and ye say, Behold a gluttonous man, and a winebibber, a friend of publicans and sinners!" The point is, sculptors and painters have represented Jesus as looking like a Nazarite with long hair parted in the middle and a beard. Greeks and Romans of that era had short hair and clean-shaven faces, though Jews in Palestine would have had beards and longer hair. Thus the early Christians in Italy would naturally portray Jesus in the styles they were familiar with, as we see at Cappella Greca.

What did Jesus look like? No one knows. The best definition I have discovered is displayed on the walls of a church in Jerusalem that displays paintings of Jesus as seen through the eyes of people from all over the earth. The paintings show Jesus as Black, Brown, Yellow, Red, and White. As you walk through this art gallery you realize again that His strong spiritual presence and unsurpassed magnetic beauty of character far exceed any physical appearance we may imagine Him to have. The Bible says that because of His message of hope for the hopeless, multitudes followed Him and forsook everything to be His disciples. The same Man and His message still attract millions today.

For Further Study

The Cambridge History of the Bible. Cambridge University Press. Ackroyd, Peter R., and Christopher F. Evans, eds. Doura.

Finegan, Jack. "Cappella Greca." *Light From the Ancient Past.* Princeton University Press, 1946.

Schaff, Philip. *History of the Christian Church.* Grand Rapids:

Just How Far Is It From Jerusalem to . . .

Amman, Jordan . . . . 56 miles
Baghdad . . . . 600 miles
Bethlehem . . . . 6 miles
Cairo . . . . 315 miles
Jericho* . . . . 18 miles
Nazareth . . . . 98 miles
New York . . . . 12 hours' flying time
Petra . . . . 220 miles
The Dead Sea† . . . . 18 miles
The Sea of Galilee . . . . 80 miles
The Mediterranean Sea‡ . . . . 36 miles

---

* Jericho is one of the oldest cities in the world. The first city to be conquered in the Promised Land, it is 830 feet below sea level and the climate is subtropical.

† The Dead Sea is called that because it is too salty to support life. Its saltiness comes from the extensive mineral deposits in the soil under it and because the sea has no outlet and thus gets so mineral-laden that its water kills all life. The countries surrounding the Dead Sea extract valuable minerals from it by evaporation.

‡ The Israeli coast along the Mediterranean Sea has a pleasant, mild climate.

Factoids About Distance, Travel, and Weather

◆ Jerusalem can have cold winds and occasionally snow in the winter, but only 15 miles east, down in the Jordan Valley, bananas and date palms grow. You can swim in the Dead Sea while, less than 20 miles away, the Mount of Olives lies under snow.

◆ It is 65 miles from the Sea of Galilee to the Dead Sea, but the Jordan River, which connects them, travels 200 miles and is one of the most crooked rivers in the world.

◆ In Jesus' time 24 miles was about one day's journey (on an animal).

◆ Bible writers often used the expression "from Dan to Beer-sheba" (from north to south) to describe the whole length of the country. This is only 140 miles as the crow flies. Measuring from west to east, it is approximately 30 miles from the Mediterranean to the Sea of Galilee and 55 miles from the Mediterranean (at Gaza) to the Dead Sea. Today the greatest distances north to south in modern Israel are 256 miles by 81 miles. The coastline is 143 miles long.

◆ According to the Pharisees of Jesus' time, a Sabbath day's journey was 2,000 cubits, or 2,916 feet, but if you stashed some food ahead of time, you could establish a residence there and therefore walk another 2,916 feet, or another 729 paces. Today it is a common sight to see a wire strung up beside the road of an Israeli village marking the legal limit one can travel outside it on Sabbath.

Surprising Facts About Angels
That Few People Know!

On July 19, 1952, Lewis and Virginia Stubbs and their two children hiked up to a fire tower on Mount Washington in New Hampshire. Virginia was pregnant and waited at the base of the tall tower while Lewis and their two sons, George, age 2, and Bob, age 4, went up to visit the ranger. Lewis carried the 2-year-old, and the 4-year-old climbed the stairs on his own. At the top Lewis reached up and knocked on the entrance opening in the floor of the tower. The ranger lifted the door, and they climbed up into the tiny observation room. Neither adult thought to close the trapdoor in the floor. Chatting with the rangers and awed by the breathtaking view, Lewis absentmindedly put the baby on the floor, not remembering that the trapdoor was open.

Seconds later, down on the ground the baby's mother sat thunderstruck as she looked up and saw her baby fall through the hole in the floor. Too frightened to scream, she watched the baby fall toward the ground—and then gently stop in midair! Suspended by unseen hands, the child neither moved, wiggled a toe, nor even cried out.

An instant later Lewis, realizing the baby had disappeared, bounded down the steps and grabbed the suspended child out of midair! Today and every day he and Virginia thank their guardian angel for saving the life of the baby.

The common definition of an angel is a supernatural being created and employed by God to communicate His will to human beings and to help and assist when they are in need. In the Old Testament angels warned Lot of the destruction of Sodom: "And there came two angels to Sodom at even: and Lot sat in the gate of Sodom: and Lot seeing them rose up to meet them" (Gen. 19:1).

However, angels are not just messengers—they can also be fierce warriors. "And it came to pass that night, that the angel of the Lord went out, and smote in the camp of the Assyrians an hundred fourscore and five thousand: and when they arose early in the morning, behold, they were all dead corpses" (2 Kings 19:35). Also, angels helped a prophet: "My God hath sent his angel, and hath shut the lions' mouths, that they have not hurt me" (Dan. 6:22).

In the New Testament angels again appear as messengers: "And when they were departed, behold, the angel of the Lord appeareth to Joseph in a dream, saying, Arise, and take the young child and his mother, and flee into Egypt" (Matt. 2:13). Also, Jesus often referred to angels, both good and evil, and to their various roles in human affairs.

Notwithstanding, certain little known facts about angels will surprise many people. The Bible never mentions angels as having wings,* and Scripture does not speak of female angels. Furthermore, angels are created beings and are

not to be worshiped; they will be judged by
human beings and are both good and evil; and
they are innumerable and do not marry.

The Old and New Testaments record the
actions of angels on behalf of humans, and they
still work for us today.

---

* The Bible does refer to creatures that have wings,
but calls them seraphim and cherubim. See Isaiah 6:2 or
Ezekiel 10:5.

Secret Books of the Bible?

What is the Bible? While that sounds like a
simple question, different people would give different answers. Jews accept only the Hebrew
Scriptures, what Christians call the Old
Testament. Protestant Christians regard the
Bible as a collection of 66 books. But Roman
Catholics and Eastern Orthodox recognize additional material as also part of the Bible. They
include as inspired the Apocrypha, a term that
comes from a Greek word meaning "hidden" or
"secret." Originally the word was used to suggest that these books contained hidden truth
that only special people could know. Scholars
classify the books of the Apocrypha into such
categories as wisdom literature, historical literature, religious romance, prophetic literature,
and legendary additions to already existing

Bible books. Some of these books got included in an ancient Greek translation of the Old Testament called the Septuagint and eventually found their way into later versions of the Bible.

Historically, the books and writings have some limited importance because they fill in the historical gap between Malachi of the Old Testament and John the Baptist of the New Testament. They supply information concerning God's people that covers the four and a half centuries called the intertestamental period (between the Old and New Testaments). However, their doctrinal content, as compared to the universally accepted books of the Bible, has long been questioned. Originally it was the Catholic scholar Jerome (died A.D. 420) who challenged their use for church doctrine and coined the title Apocrypha to describe such writings.

Later Martin Luther also doubted the content of the apocryphal books and had them placed in a group at the end of the German Old Testament. He objected to such teachings of the Apocrypha as the doctrine of purgatory and the supposed benefit of prayers for the dead (2 Maccabees 12:43-45). Also, Luther took exception to their emphasis on the merit of good works for salvation (Tobit 12:9; Ecclesiasticus 3:33; etc.).

Today the Apocrypha still remains in dispute. In 1546 the Catholic Church, at the Council of Trent, officially overruled the earlier objections of Jerome and declared them as part of their Holy Scriptures. Such official Catholic translations as the Douay-Rheims Bible (1609) include the Apocrypha inter-spersed among the rest of the canonical books.

Following Martin Luther's lead, the Protestant churches do not accept the books of the Apocrypha as inspired. They feel that the teachings of prayers for the dead and a number of other ideas are not consistent with the New Testament. In 1827 the British and Foreign Bible Society stopped including the Apocrypha in the Bibles they printed; the American Bible Society soon began doing the same. However, it can be found as supplemental material in spe-cial editions of *The New English Bible* and the New Revised Standard Version.

For Further Study

Unger, Merrill. "The Apocrypha of the Old Testament." *Introductory Guide to the Old Testament.* Grand Rapids: Zondervan.

Is Jesus Mentioned Outside the Bible?

People are often puzzled by the fact that nonbiblical writers who lived during the same time as Jesus do not mention Him. But this should come as no surprise when you consider the short span of Jesus' earthly ministry and His emphasis on the kingdom to come. Even His own disciples misunderstood His true mis-

sion and expected Him to lead a great uprising
to liberate His people and usher in a kingdom
on earth. To the Greek and Roman writers
Jesus was just an insignificant flicker in the
history of an unimportant nation and people.
They would have considered Him as just one
of many so-called messiahs who had come to
liberate the Jewish people.

However, a few early extrabiblical references do appear to speak of Jesus. While the
only reliable references to Jesus occur in the
Scriptures, about 50 false gospels, or books
about Jesus, competed with the genuine Gospels
of Matthew, Mark, Luke, and John. Some of
these books exist only as fragments, and others
only by name. They date back only to the second
century or later.

Keeping in mind that while many mentions
of Jesus outside of the Bible are suspect for
various reasons, the writings of the Jewish historian and turncoat general Josephus (he
joined the Roman side after being captured by
them) are accepted as genuine. He says of
Jesus: "Now, there was about this time, Jesus,
a wise man, if it be lawful to call Him a man,
for He was doer of wonderful works—a
teacher of such men as receive the truth with
pleasure. He drew over to Him both many of
the Jews, and many of the Gentiles. He was
[the] Christ; and when Pilate, at the suggestion
of the principal men amongst us, had condemned Him to the cross, those that loved Him

at the first did not forsake Him, for He appeared to them alive again the third day, as the divine prophets had foretold these and ten thousand other wonderful things concerning Him; and the tribe of Christians, so named from Him, are not extinct at this day."

Many feel that Josephus' account is partly his and partly the work of a Christian who rewrote some of it in more favorable terms.

Allusions to Jesus in the writings of the Greeks and Romans are either nonexistent or highly suspect. For instance, there is the supposed testimony of Mara, a philosopher, to his son Serapio in about A.D. 74. Speaking of the deaths of Socrates and Pythagoras, Mara remarks, ". . . or the Jews [by the murder] of their Wise King, seeing that from that very time their kingdom was driven away [from them]?"

Cornelius Tacitus, the great Roman historian (died about A.D. 117), in giving an account of the Neronian persecution, attests that Jesus was put to death as a criminal by Pontius Pilate in the reign of emperor Tiberius and that He founded the Christian sect. Tacitus characterizes Christianity as arising in Judea and spreading in spite of Christ's disgraceful death. Christianity encountered such hatred and contempt throughout the empire that a "vast multitude" of believers were cruelly put to death in the city of Rome alone as early as the year A.D. 64.

For Further Study

Bruce, F. F. *Jesus and Christian Origins Outside the New Testament.* Grand Rapids: Eerdmans, 1974.

"Jesus Christ." *World Book Encyclopedia.*

Josephus, Flavius. *Complete Works.* Translated by William Whiston. Grand Rapids: Kregel Publications. P. 379.

Schaff, Philip. *History of the Christian Church.* Vol. 1, pp. 94 and 171.

The Bible and Supernatural Guidance

Life-and-death decisions have always prompted human beings to try to divine their futures. Some methods have been bizarre. For instance, we read in Ezekiel 21:21: "The king of Babylonia stands by the signpost at the fork of the road. To discover which way to go, he shakes the arrows, he consults his idols; he examines the liver of a sacrificed animal. Now! His right hand holds the arrow marked 'Jerusalem'" (TEV).

The Babylonian king did three things to try to find an answer. First he shook some arrows with appropriate messages written on them and made one to fall out of the quiver. Next he consulted some small idols, called teraphim, in some unknown manner, and finally he looked at an animal's liver. This last act of divination was an ancient practice of cutting open an animal's liver and discerning a message from the shape of the organ. The interpretation came from comparing it with special model livers made of clay.

In other instances pagan astrologers and magicians would try to read the future by watching flights of birds or pouring oil on water and watching it spread. Somehow it all sounds like the grandparent of reading tarot cards and tea leaves, and crystal gazing.

It wasn't just the pagan kings who sought to learn the future. God's people also had methods to determine what was the best choice. For example, 1 Samuel 14:41 tells of a case in which King Saul attempted to determine guilt by casting lots. A New Testament example of casting lots appears in Acts 1:26, in which the apostles choose a replacement for Judas. No one knows for sure what "casting lots" was, or the exact method used. It is assumed that some small objects—stones or clay tablets, perhaps—were used to indicate God's approval or disapproval.

In another instance David sought God's guidance on a military decision. He ordered a priest to bring an object called the ephod. First Samuel 30:7, 8 records: "Bring me hither the ephod. And Abiathar brought thither the ephod to David. And David enquired at the Lord, saying, Shall I pursue after this troop? Shall I overtake them? And he answered him, Pursue." It is unclear how the ephod worked. It may have been the vest-type object that the high priest wore on his chest called the ephod of gold. Considered the most sacred part of the priest's clothing, it held the high priestly breastplate and two objects called the Urim and Thummim.

The breastplate was about 10 inches square and had 12 heavy gems attached to it. Each stone represented one of the tribes of Israel. In addition, perhaps in a pocket that rested over the heart of the priest, were the Urim and Thummim. Straps over the shoulders of the high priest supported the breastplate. No one is certain how the Urim and Thummim worked, but it is clear that they were used to indicate the will of God. The last mention of their use appears in Ezra 2:63.

Why We Can Trust the Accuracy of the Bible

We sat in a large circle, and someone whispered a phrase or sentence into the ear of the first person. That person passed it to the next, and so the message went around the whole circle. The last person then repeated what he had heard out loud for all to hear. The results were hilarious, as the final version barely resembled how it had begun. Word of mouth is at best inaccurate, and handwritten messages can get garbled.

Accuracy in communication during ancient times was not an easy task. Without computers, laser printers, and copy machines, the writer's life in Jesus' time was a genuine ordeal. Early manuscripts had to be written out entirely in longhand with a crude ink pen on a roll of rough paper or animal skin. The apostle Paul often dictated his thoughts to a male secretary, called a scribe, who would write them on a scroll that could be as long as 35 feet. Romans 16:22 reads: "I Tertius [Paul's scribe for this book], who wrote this epistle, salute you in the Lord." Here Paul wanted to share his thoughts with a number of churches, and therefore he had to have copies made.

People wishing to have copies of a letter or other document made would take the original to a scriptorium. This equivalent of a modern-day publishing house employed professional copyists called scribes. For quick jobs requiring a number of copies, a foreman would stand before several scribes and read the manuscript out loud. Although this was the fastest method, it was the least accurate way of copying. For more serious matters, such as the sacred thoughts of an apostle, one single scribe would copy from an original manuscript word for word. He would repeat the process again and again, constantly comparing his work with the original manuscript to ensure that the copy was as accurate as humanly possible. After its completion, the copy would be carefully checked by a proofreader, perhaps even by the author himself. The original copy was called the autograph. Today no autographs of the Holy Scriptures are known to exist.

The discovery of the Dead Sea scrolls in 1947 testifies to the accuracy and dedication of the people who hand-copied the Holy Scriptures over the years. Three Bedouin herdsmen tending their sheep near a place called Wadi Qumran found the first of the scrolls. One of them playfully tossed a rock into an opening in a nearby cliff. He heard the stone strike something that sounded like pottery. Two of them lowered the third into the opening, and he found what would become one of the greatest archaeological discoveries of all time. Eventually archaeologists explored 11 caves that yielded some 600 manuscripts, 200 of them biblical material. The 50,000 to 60,000 manuscript fragments include every book of the Old Testament except Esther.

Some of the materials date back as far as 250 B.C. and confirm the accuracy of our present Old Testament Scriptures. Indeed, you can trust the accuracy of the Bible because God has inspired individuals of all ages to preserve the Holy Scriptures carefully.

For Deeper Study

Ackroyd, Peter R., and Christopher F. Evans, eds. "From the Beginnings to Jerome" and "Books in the Graeco-Roman World and in the New Testament." *The Cambridge History of the Bible.* Cambridge University Press.

Comfort, Philip Wesley. "The Dead Sea Scrolls." *The Origin of the Bible.* Wheaton, Ill. Tyndale House Publishers, 1992.

_____ . *The Quest for the Original Text of the New Testament.* Grand Rapids: Baker Book House, 1992. P. 55.

Amazing Statistics

The Bible is a truly extraordinary collection of books and letters written by at least 36 different authors. The writers include prophets, fishermen, kings, missionaries, a lawyer, priests, a doctor, and a tax collector. The Bible spans some 1,600 years, divided into two basic periods — the Old Testament, written before Christ, and the New Testament, composed after Him.

Scholars divided the books of the Bible into chapters and verses to make references easier to find. The King James Version of the Bible contains 1,189 chapters, 929 in the Old Testament and 260 in the New Testament. The longest division is Psalm 119, with 176 verses, and the shortest is Psalm 117, with only 33 words. The middle of the Bible is Psalm 117. The books of Jude, Obadiah, Philemon, and 2 and 3 John are only one chapter long.

The English Bible has 31,101 verses. The Old Testament contains 23,144 verses, the New Testament 7,957. The middle verse of the Bible is Psalm 103:2, which is verse number 15,551 of 31,101. The shortest verse is "Jesus wept" (John 11:35), and the longest is Esther 8:9.

Originally the Bible had no chapter or verse divisions. Instead, the texts were simply large blocks of letters all written side by side. The Hebrew had a dot or space between words, and the Greek of the New Testament did not have any break between words at all. One can easily imagine the difficulty of trying to figure out where one word ended and the next began. To understand the kind of problem the reader had to deal with, consider the following English sentence run together, as the original Greek text often would be: "Godisnowhere." Is it "God is nowhere" or "God is now here"? It makes a big difference how you break the letters apart into words. Nor was there any punctuation separating one sentence or thought from another. In addition, trying to refer to a specific passage was extremely difficult. You almost had to have the text already memorized before you could know how it should be read.

However, some progress was made when early manuscripts made for public reading were written in larger print with reading aids such as punctuation, breathing marks, and blank spaces for paragraphs. But it was still more than 1,200 years after the beginning of the Christian Era before anyone divided the Bible into chapters. Chapter divisions are usually credited to the work of Stephen Langton, archbishop of Canterbury, in England, who died in 1228.

A printer from Paris made the division into verses, as we find the arrangement today, about the year 1550. Tradition says he did it while making a horseback journey from Lyons to Paris. The first English New Testament broken into verses was published in 1557 and three years later the entire Bible.

We should note that neither the chapter

and verse divisions nor the punctuation is inspired. However, the idea of dividing the Scriptures into chapters proved to be so convenient that Jewish scholars adopted the idea. Therefore, the present-day Hebrew Scriptures have chapter divisions similar to the English Old Testament.

In one year you can read the entire Bible by reading a little more than three chapters per day.

Some of the
Best-known Chapters of the Bible

1. The love chapter................1 Corinthians 13
2. The faith chapter......................Hebrews 11
3. The resurrection chapter .....1 Corinthians 15
4. The twenty-third psalm.................Psalm 23
5. The forgiveness psalm ....Psalm 51
6. The Suffering Servant chapter......Isaiah 53
7. The heaven chapter................Revelation 21

The name Jesus Christ appears in the first and last verses of the New Testament.

The famous inscription on the Liberty Bell in Independence Hall, Philadelphia, came from Leviticus 25:10: "Proclaim liberty throughout all the land unto all the inhabitants thereof."

For Deeper Study

Comfort, Philip Wesley. *The Quest for the Original Text of the New Testament.*
_____. *The Origin of the Bible.*

Greenslade, S. L., ed. "The West From the Reformation to the Present Day." *The Cambridge History of the Bible.* Cambridge University Press, 1963.

The Mysterious Books Rejected by All Faiths

The books of the pseudepigrapha (a term meaning false [pseudo] writings [pigrapha]) have been rejected as false by Jews, Catholics, and Protestants alike. They consist of a variety of books written by Jews and others from 200 B.C. to A.D. 200 on religious subjects. Many of the books claim to be written by famous persons of the biblical past. A couple examples are: the Book of Adam and Eve; Testaments of the Twelve Patriarchs.

Anyone who reads them will quickly reject them as uninspired. The following excerpt from the Acts of John illustrates the point: "Now on the first day we arrived at a deserted inn, and when we were at a loss for a bed for John, we saw a droll matter. There was one bedstead lying somewhere there without coverings, whereon we spread the cloaks which we were wearing, and we prayed him to lie down upon it and rest, while the rest of us all slept upon the floor. But he when he lay down was troubled by the bugs, and as they continued to become yet more troublesome to him, when it was now about the middle of the night, in the hearing of us all he said to

them: I say unto you, O bugs, behave yourselves, one and all, and leave your abode for this
night and remain quiet in one place, and keep
your distance from the servants of God. And as
we laughed, and went on talking for some time,
John addressed himself to sleep; and we, talking
low, gave him no disturbance. . . .

"But when the day was now dawning I arose
first, and with me Verus and Andronicus, and we
saw at the door of the house which we had taken
a great number of bugs standing, and while we
wondered at the great sight of them, and all the
brethren were roused up because of them, John
continued sleeping. And when he was awaked
we declared to him what we had seen. And he sat
up on the bed and looked at them and said: Since
ye have well behaved yourselves in hearkening to
my rebuke, come unto your place. And when he
had said this, and risen from the bed, the bugs
running from the door hasted to the bed and
climbed up by the legs thereof and disappeared
into the joints. And John said again: This crea-
ture hearkened unto the voice of a man, and
abode by itself and was quiet and trespassed not;
but we which hear the voice and commandments
of God disobey and are light-minded: and for
how long?" (verses 60, 61).

For Further Study

Ackroyd, Peter R., and Christopher F. Evans, eds.
"Pseudepigrapha." *The Cambridge History of the Bible.*

James, M. R., trans. *The Apocryphal New Testament.* Oxford
Press.

Why and How to Study the Bible

In order to study the Bible, we must begin by understanding that the Bible is not a textbook, a history book, or a set of lessons all laid out in a simple fashion. Instead, the Bible is a collection of 66 books written over a span of 1,600 years by a number of authors. The Bible contains "salvation history," historical accounts of God working through His people to do His will. In short, the Bible is ultimately about Jesus the Messiah and Saviour. The Old Testament people looked forward in faith to His day. In our day we look backward in faith to His life and the instructions He gave His followers. And in faith we all look forward to His coming again.

Why study the Bible? The psalmist compared the Word of God to a light to guide us through this dark world. "Thy word is a lamp unto my feet, and a light unto my path" (Ps. 119:105). Jesus asks us to "search the scriptures; for in them ye think ye have eternal life: and they are they which testify of me" (John 5:39). Furthermore, Paul the apostle remarked to his young friend Timothy, "Study to shew thyself approved of God, a workman that needeth not to be ashamed, rightly dividing the word of truth" (2 Tim. 2:15), and then further reminded him that "all scripture is given by inspiration of God, and is profitable for doctrine, for reproof, for correction, for instruction in righteousness" (2 Tim. 3:16).

Of course, applying the principle of what Jesus and Paul were saying, we today should search and study the Bible and in it find instruction for living both in the present life and in the life forever after.

How Do We Study the Bible?

Begin with prayer. Ask God to give you wisdom and understanding as you open His Holy Word. If you are new to the Bible, don't start with the Gospel of Matthew and the "begats." Instead, turn to the Gospel of Mark, which is only 16 chapters long. Next move on to the 21 chapters of the Gospel of John. However, take notice of how each book begins. Mark starts his account of the life of Jesus with the career of John the Baptist, while the disciple John goes all the way back to the beginning of time. On the other hand, Matthew heads his Gospel with an all-important list of the family line of Jesus, while Dr. Luke's Gospel begins with the parents of John the Baptist. We have four different writers telling of the life and times of Jesus from four differing points of view.

Next read the Acts of the Apostles and learn in more detail what happened in the lives of the followers of Jesus after His crucifixion. Once you have completed it, you can move on into the Epistles, or Letters, of the New Testament. It is vitally important that you remember that you are reading only one side of the story. In many cases the Bible writer has written the letter in response to some problem in a church that he has heard about. For instance, in Galatians 1:6 the apostle Paul comments: "I marvel that ye are so soon removed from him that called you into the grace of Christ unto another gospel."

Obviously Paul is upset because word has gotten back to him that the Galatian church has big problems. Paul thunders at them, "O foolish Galatians, who hath bewitched you, that ye should not obey the truth?" (Gal. 3:1). In yet another instance he writes to the Corinthian church. "For first of all, when ye come together in the church, I hear that there be divisions among you; and I partly believe it" (1 Cor. 11:18).

The examples cited above point out that the reader will find that much of the New Testament was directed to individual churches or people groups of the time. Certainly Paul's thunderings were not meant specifically for us today, but we can apply the principles he laid down to modern life. Someone has said that history doesn't repeat itself, but human nature does! What Scripture has to say about death, sorrow, disease, illness, lying, cheating, stealing, gossiping, adultery, and all of the infinite aspects of sin applies to us today just as it did to the Christians of the first century. Likewise, the Old Testament is full of people stories and lessons we can use in our daily lives. It shows how God demonstrates His love and works in the lives of His people.

How Did the Bible Get Its Name?

The word *Bible* does not occur in the Holy Scriptures. The English word *Bible* came from the Greek word for the papyrus plant that the Egyptians used to make paper. The Greeks called the plant *biblos,* and eventually writing products derived from the plant, such as scrolls, also became known as *biblos.* The ancient Phoenician city of Byblos derived its name from its extensive manufacture of and trade in writing materials.

The Greeks still use the term *biblos* today. During a trip through customs at the Athens airport in Greece the author had to register some ancient pottery he was transporting from Israel to a museum in the U.S.A. As we sat in a little side office in the airport, I watched the customs officer reach over to a stack of record books that he had hand-labeled biblos and then enter the pertinent information.

Additionally, among the terms the sacred writers employed to designate the collection of books that we call the Bible are the Scriptures, the Holy Scriptures, the Word, the Word of Truth, and the law and the prophets. During the time it took to compose all the books of the Bible the various writings circulated individually or in groups. It was not until the fourth century A.D. that the books were all put in a single volume.

The Name They Would Not Say

Did you know that when you open the King James Version of the Bible as well as some other translations you will find a name that exists today only because people forgot how to pronounce another name?

When God instructed Moses to lead the children of Israel out of Egypt, the Hebrew leader asked God who he should say had sent him. God replied, "Thus shalt thou say unto the children of Israel, I AM hath sent me unto you" (Ex. 3:14).

We can transliterate the Hebrew words for I AM as YHWH. Ancient Hebrew writing did not include written vowels such as the English a, e, i, o, and u. They wrote their language only with consonants. When they read a Hebrew word out loud, they simply added in the necessary vowel sounds as they spoke. However, when they read YHWH, they in time gave it special treatment. Instead of adding in the vowels, the speaker substituted a whole new word or simply left it blank. This was because of the sacredness they attached to the word YHWH and their fear of profaning the name of God. Therefore, the reader would often say the word "Lord" instead of YHWH when reading it. This worked well until the use of the ancient Hebrew language died out. People forgot what vowels were to be used when they pronounced the words.

In the seventh century, to preserve their ancient language, a group of Jewish scholars called the Masoretes inserted vowels with the words. However, when they came to YHWH they included the vowels for the word "Lord" ("Adonai" in the Hebrew). Translators of the English Bible from the twelfth century on unknowingly made the combination of the two words into the new word "Jehovah" (YHWH plus the vowels from Adonai). The word "Jehovah" is an invention of the English Bible translators based on the consonants of one word and the vowels of another.

The word YHWH occurs more than 6,800 times in the Old Testament. The King James translators generally rendered the word as "Lord." However, examples of YHWH translated as "Jehovah" appear in Exodus 6:3, Psalm 83:18, and Isaiah 12:2. It is ironic that today the proper pronunciation of the word still remains a mystery. The one word that people would not dare say has now become the word they cannot say.

Will I Know You in Heaven?

According to the Bible, yes!

What a loss heaven would be if it were a community of strangers without a past. If heaven is anything less than we now know, who would want to go there? Paul states the Christian hope when he says, "We, however, are citizens of heaven, and we eagerly wait for our Savior, the Lord Jesus Christ, to come from heaven. He will change our weak mortal bodies and make them like his own glorious body, using that power by which he is able to bring all things under his rule" (Phil. 3:20, 21, TEV).

Also, in a letter to the Corinthian church members, Paul said, "For when the trumpet sounds, the dead will be raised, never to die again, and we shall all be changed. For what is mortal must be changed into what is immortal; what will die must be changed into what cannot die" (1 Cor. 15:52, 53, TEV). Of course, deformities and birth defects will vanish, but our characters and personalities, as transformed by the Holy Spirit into Christ's likeness, will remain. We will be able to recognize each other just as we often know childhood friends when we meet them years later as adults.

The Bible and the Seven-Day Week

First, a quick review of something you already know. The earth rotates on its axis once every 24 hours. We call that span of time one day. Next the moon circles the earth once every 30 days. So we term that period of time a "moonth," or a month. Finally, the earth orbits the sun once every 365 days, and we label it a year.

As you can easily understand, these divisions of time come about quite naturally, and humanity has known and used them since ancient times. But where did the seven-day week come from? What natural phenomena is it based on? Why not an eight-, nine-, 10-, or even 12-day week?

Anthropologists have uncovered some interesting clues. They have found that indeed some cultures tried using weeks of various lengths. Some tribes in West Africa adopted a week a mere four days long, but it didn't last. During Napoleon's time the French government experimented with a 10-day week. But like all the others, the standard seven-day week soon returned. Science has still not answered why human beings prefer a seven-day week. However, there is an answer, but it is found in the Bible — and the Bible only!

"And on the seventh day God ended his work which he had made. . . . And God blessed the seventh day, and sanctified it: because that in it he had rested from all his work which God created and made" (Gen. 2:2, 3). So there it is — the origin of the seven-day cycle that we call a week. However, we still haven't answered the question "Why did God make this repeating cycle of days we now call a week?" Some suggest that it was His way of repeating again and again to an often-forgetful human family that they should remember their roots!

Perhaps we can better understand this point by looking at some of the extraordinary ways people have tried to leave a memory of themselves to the world. Egypt's pharaohs, for example, erected huge monuments called obelisks, on which they inscribed the details of their battles and other achievements.

The Greeks used marble and bronze to produce likenesses of heroes, athletes, and philosophers. The Romans made a practice of preserving wax masks of ancestors and also hired sculptors to make personal statues to display in front of their homes. Even today several thousand dollars for an elaborate cemetery headstone is not uncommon.

From the pharaohs to the present time, monuments, statues, and markers have had basically the same intent—to enable the world to remember us. Could the seven-day week be one of God's methods of reminding us to remember Him, our Creator?

Suppose you had the challenge to make a permanent marker to remind all people that they were to forever remember and respect their Creator. Yes, you could have the message chiseled in stone, but it would have to resist the constant effects of weathering. Even if it survived the forces of nature, it would still be subject, as were the pharaohs' monuments, to human tampering. History tells us that conquerors often thought nothing of chiseling out a predecessor's achievements and changing battle accounts to suit themselves. No, it seems a stone marker, no matter how large, would not suffice.

God knew the best way. He set up a commemorative marker of time by creating the seven-day week. His idea of stringing seven days like beads on the strand of time is so unique that human beings can never claim the idea to be of natural origin, linked in some way with the moon, sun, or stars. Furthermore, we can see that the seven-day week exists entirely because of the Sabbath day.

The Sabbath is like a period at the end of a sentence—it tells you when to stop. It is the period at the end of the week. Six ordinary days pass, and then the Sabbath punctuates the week and says, "Stop here." The seven-day week exists only because God appointed the Sabbath day to mark its conclusion. All the other days of the week are so ordinary that the Bible simply numbers them as first, second, third, etc. Thus the evidence seems abundant that the only source of the seven-day week is the supernatural work of God the Creator.

So far we have addressed only the first half of the problem. With the week ending every seventh day, it shouldn't be difficult to remember the Creator, but what about respecting Him? Once again God knew best. After the work was done, He carefully set aside the last day of the week, blessed that day, and made it a time of rest. To make sure that we understood its purpose and function, God gave these instructions:

"Remember the Sabbath day by keeping it holy. Six days you shall labor and do all your work, but the seventh day is a Sabbath to the Lord your God. On it you shall not do any work, neither you, nor your son or daughter, nor your manservant or maidservant, nor your animals, nor the alien within your gates. For in six days the Lord made the heavens and the earth, the sea, and all that is in them, but he rested on the seventh day. Therefore the Lord blessed the Sabbath day and made it holy" (Ex. 20:8-11, NIV).

Now we can see the Creator's reasoning more clearly. First He put up stop signs along the road of time—one every seven days. Next He provided an oasis beside the hot, dusty road; planted it with tall, waving palm trees; beautified it with cool, reflecting pools; and caressed it with gentle, living waters and acres of green grass and flowers planted by quiet walkways. Finally the Creator asks life's travelers to come in, rest for a day, leave the world outside, and allow themselves to be refreshed physically and spiritually.

Isn't it puzzling that the only things that last are the things we cannot touch, taste, hear, smell, or see? The apostle Paul calls them the invisible things of the world. The seven-day week and the reason it exists—the Sabbath day—are invisible, unchangeable markers on the unseen stream of time. Their existence will continue on into the era when the earth is made new.

The seven-day week and the Sabbath will always remain a mystery for some. But those who accept God's initiation to enter its oasis understand that God's holy Sabbath and the seven-day week began in Eden, continue today, and are a definite part of the future and forever.

For Further Study

"Time." *World Book Encyclopedia*.

How Did They Decide Which Books to Include in the Bible?

The Jewish Bible has 39 books, most of the Protestant Bibles have 66, and the Catholic Bible includes 73 books. Of course, the Jews do not accept the New Testament, because they do not believe Jesus of Nazareth to be the Messiah. The Protestants and Catholics disagree only over what is to be included in the Old Testament. The difference is over the *canon*, or the list of the books of the Holy Scriptures accepted as inspired and part of the Bible.

It is said that at the end of the first century the Jewish rabbis in the councils of Jamnia (A.D. 90 and 118) agreed on which of the Hebrew books they felt measured up to be considered authoritative. In reality, they were only confirming what had already been accepted by the faithful. (Scholars increasingly question whether any such Jamnia councils ever took place at all.) We do know that after this period the questions of which books should be officially included in the Old Testament were no longer considered to be of any consequence. Four criteria were thought to be considered in any deliberations about what books to include: (1) the book must have originated between the time of Moses and Ezra, when inspiration was believed to have begun and ended; (2) what was presented in the books must be in harmony with the Law (the first five books of Moses: Genesis, Exodus, Leviticus, Numbers, and Deuteronomy); (3) the language of the original book should be Hebrew; and generally (4) they should have been written within the geographical limits of Palestine. In many ways these criteria were arguments why people thought a book was canonical rather than reasons for selecting it in the first place. The Holy Spirit had already convinced God's people which books were inspired.

During its early years the Christian church came to recognize 27 more books as measuring up to the canon or standard. They also had four basic tests they used to determine whether to include a writing. The criteria were: (1) the book should be written by an apostle or by a person with such a close relationship with the early church leaders that the book would be of an apostolic caliber; (2) the book was to give clear evidence that it was divinely inspired; (3) the book was to be universally accepted by the church; (4) the contents of the book were to be in harmony with other Scripture and of a high spiritual nature. The Third Council of Carthage in A.D. 397 seems to have agreed that the 27 books of the New Testament we have today measured up for use in the church.

"It is a remarkable fact that no early church council selected the books that should constitute the New Testament canon. The books that we now have crushed out all rivals, not by any adventitious authority, but by their own weight and worth," declares Henry Thiessen in his book *Introduction to the New Testament.*

It should be made clear that Protestants believe that God's Word, as written in books, is self-authenticating. Through the leading of the Holy Spirit, people knew which books were and were not inspired. In other words, the very content of the book spoke for itself. God's Holy Word did not need a group of scholars to declare it acceptable. The councils merely agreed with what the community of believers, under the guidance of the Holy Spirit, had already accepted.

For Further Study

Thiessen, Henry. "Canon of the N.T." *Introduction to the New Testament.* Grand Rapids: William Eerdmans Publishing.

Comfort, Philip Wesley. *The Origin of the Bible.*

Unger, Merrill F. "Jamnia." *Guide to the Old Testament.* Grand Rapids: Zondervan.

The Difficulty of Bible Translation

Communication was much easier back when, according to Genesis 11:1, "the whole earth was of one language, and of one speech." It is often difficult enough to get an idea across to someone when we speak the same language, but it becomes even more of a problem when we use different languages. I learned this first-hand when the Army stationed me in Germany and I decided to learn the language.

To begin, I bought a German/English dictionary, which I carried with me everywhere I went. I made notes, listened carefully, and even dressed like a German to disguise myself. Through hard work and lots of practice I improved quickly. However, my teacher told me that I would really master the language only when I learned to think in German. Of course, this is true for any language. You have to learn to think like the people do and use the things they are familiar with. For instance, in English I would say "My car sits outside," while in German I would say "My car stands outside." Either way, the car is outside, but how one thinks determines whether it is sitting or standing.

This may seem like a trivial matter until we translate the Bible from one language and culture to another. For example, how would you explain to Inuits about sheep and lambs and Jesus being the Lamb of God? They have never seen sheep. In another part of the world, how would you present Psalm 23 to a group of African cattle herders who consider sheep a nuisance?

Reactions to misunderstood information can sometimes turn to violence. Some years ago, near Cumming, Georgia, irate Native Americans burned a church to the ground. They said the preacher was a liar for having told the preposterous story of Jonah and the fish. They surmised that the man was insulting their intelligence because everyone knew fish don't grow large enough to swallow people!

In his book *Message and Mission*, Eugene Albert Nida says that linguists "have . . . demonstrated that anything said in any language can be communicated in another, though often with greatly altered ways of speaking." However, regardless of the difficulty, the work of translating the gospel of Jesus Christ continues in ever-widening circles. As of December 31, 1993, the Bible had been translated into 2,062 languages. It is complete in 337 of these languages, 799 have the New Testament, and the rest have one or more books.

For Further Study

Ackroyd, Peter R., and Christopher F. Evans, eds. "From Beginnings to Jerome" and "The Gutenberg Bible." *The Cambridge History of the Bible.*

Comfort, Philip Wesley. *The Origin of the Bible.* P. 233.

Schaff, Philip. "Luther's Translation of the Bible." *History of the Christian Church.*

What About All of Those Bible Translations?

The Bible was not originally written in English. The authors of the Old Testament wrote mostly in Hebrew, the ancient language of the Jews. The New Testament appeared in the Greek spoken by the common people of that day.

A very small part of the Old Testament — portions of Ezra and Daniel — uses a language called Aramaic. However, by the time of Jesus, the Aramaic language was widely used by the Jews as well as Greek and Hebrew. Closely related to Hebrew, it became like a sister tongue to the Jewish people and was employed in a way similar to how the English language often works today. A German and a Chinese, for example, may use English to talk to each other just as the Jews spoke Aramaic to communicate with the non-Jewish world around them.

Because of a decline in the use of ancient Hebrew, especially among the Jews living outside of Palestine, the Egyptian Jews often used a Bible translated into Greek. Called the Septuagint, it was completed in Alexandria, Egypt, about 130 B.C. When Jesus, the apostles, or the New Testament writers quote the Old Testament, they are often citing this Greek translation. Jesus repeatedly asked the people, "Have you not read?" and then He continued His sermon as if He knew full well that they were familiar with the same holy writings as He. However, the scriptures He quoted were from the Septuagint (scholars often abbreviate it as the LXX, or 70, from the tradition that 70-some translators worked on it).

Christianity was born into a world controlled by the Romans, who spoke Latin and Greek. Latin was their language, but Greek was their adopted language of learning and culture, and formed a part of an educated Roman's training. Latin was probably limited to government, military, and legal use, while Greek was the more widely used common language of the then-known world. Referring to the placard put on Jesus' cross, John 19:20 reads: "This title then read many of the Jews: for the place where Jesus was crucified was nigh to the city and it was written in Hebrew, and Greek, and Latin."

As the centuries passed, Latin replaced Greek as the official language in the Christian church. Therefore, it became necessary to translate the Bible into official Latin. Jerome, a Roman Catholic scholar who died in A.D. 420, produced the Latin Vulgate, a version that would be the Roman Catholic standard for more than 1,000 years. The French in the 1100s, the Italians and Spanish in the 1200s, and the German and English in the 1300s made attempts to translate the Bible into their native languages.

Jerome's Latin Vulgate Bible is said to be the first book printed from movable type and is called "the Gutenberg Bible." The first printing was finished in 1455, and 40 copies of it still exist. It is estimated that for a person of the time to buy this Bible on vellum (animal skin) was the equivalent cost of buying a house today.

Some Early English Translations

John Wycliffe (died 1384) was an English Catholic priest. Often called "the Morning Star of the Reformation," he translated from the Latin Vulgate to produce the first extensive rendering of the Scriptures in English. His translation became the basis of Protestant thought in England even though the authorities banned the common people from reading it and burned all copies of it whenever possible. Because it was a translation of a translation, its accuracy was not as good as it could have been. It is a small book, which was unusual for its time, and was copied by hand.

William Tyndale (died 1536) translated from the original Greek and is often called the "Father of the English Bible." Because the English banned his translation, he published it in Europe and smuggled it into England. Captured by the authorities, he was eventually strangled (as was the custom of the times for mercy's sake) and burned at the stake as a heretic in 1536. His final prayer was "Lord, open the king of England's eyes." Scholars estimate that 90 percent of the King James Version of the New Testament is his work.

Miles Coverdale (died 1568) was an English bishop. He translated the first complete

English Bible to come from a printing press, though he borrowed largely from Tyndale's work, including all of the Old Testament and much of the New Testament. His version was popularly known as the "Bugs Bible" because of its reading of Psalm 91:5: "Thou shalt not nede to be afraid of any bugges by night."

The Geneva Bible (1560), published by English religious exiles, is often called "the Breeches Bible" because it describes the original garments of Adam and Eve as breeches: "And they sewed fig leaves together, and made themselves breeches." It was the first English Bible divided into chapters and verses. This Bible, considered the most scholarly of the early versions, served for 75 years and was the family Bible of the English people. It was a strong competitor with the King James Version.

The Roman Catholic Douay-Rheims Bible (1609) was a direct translation into English from the Latin Vulgate, the official Bible of the Roman Catholic Church. The Roman Catholic college at Rheims, France, which later moved to Douay, France, undertook the translation from the Latin. Thus it is called the Douay-Rheims Version and is a translation of a translation.

The English monarch allowed it because of the offensive doctrinal notes that appeared in the margins of other Bibles such as the Geneva Bible. Historically, it was a time of opposition to the outright authority of the English king, and many of the margin notes spoke against kingship. People often referred to the margin comments as "bitter notes." Many term the King James Version as a "version" instead of a translation because it was supposed to have been a revision of the already existing Bibles. The English scholars assigned to it had freedom to use any parts of earlier translations that they found acceptable. It took seven years for the 54 scholars, mostly professors in English universities, to finish their work. No translation has surpassed the literary beauty and popularity of the King James Version. Yet it was not popular at first, because the people favored the Geneva Bible. Also, it was physically immense, weighing more than 20 pounds.

For Deeper Study

Ackroyd, Peter R., and Christopher F. Evans, eds. "From Beginnings to Jerome" and "About the Gutenberg Bible." *The Cambridge History of the Bible.*

Comfort, Philip Wesley. "Bible Translation." *The Origin of the Bible.*

Schaff, Philip. "The German Reformation" and "Luther's Translation of the Bible." *History of the Christian Church.*

The Church the Bible Founded

The Christian church has its roots in the Hebrew Scriptures and Judaism, the religion of its people. For centuries the Jews hoped for the coming of their promised Messiah. By the time of Jesus, conditions for the Jewish nation had gone from bad to worse. Their tiny kingdom struggled under the thumb of the pagan Roman Empire, which had appointed a king they despised. Herod the Great, king of the Jews, was called "the king of a nation that hated him."

Although the Jews longed for their promised deliverer, they were actually looking for a great military leader to liberate them from Rome's hated rule. Instead, God had other plans, as the apostle Paul says: "But when the right time finally came, God sent his own Son. He came as the son of a human mother and lived under the Jewish Law, to redeem those who were under the Law, so that we might become God's sons" (Gal. 4:4, 5, TEV).

When Jesus, God in the flesh, walked among the Jews and taught them of a heavenly kingdom to come, many rejected Him because He did not meet their expectations. Jesus emphasized that in order to be citizens of the kingdom of God, people needed to transform from the inside out. In part, His point was that merely changing their living circumstances on earth was not a permanent solution. Jesus taught that a human being is born a sinner and needs a divine rescue in order to be saved. But the Jews wanted a powerful warrior king. Ironically, though, when Pilate, the Roman governor, asked, "Shall I crucify your King?" the mob replied, "We have no king but Caesar" (John 19:15).

In their violent opposition to the teachings and claims of Jesus, a number of the Jewish leaders had Him murdered.

During a brief public ministry lasting approximately three years, Jesus put in place a work that would turn the world upside down. So revolutionary would be His impact upon humanity that much of the world today measures time as B.C. (before Christ) and A.D. *(anno Domini,* in the year of the Lord since the beginning of the Christian Era). Even the Jews, rejecting the A.D./B.C. notations, indirectly acknowledge Christ's existence by their use of B.C.E. (before the Common Era) to measure time. The Common Era is the Christian Era.

After Christ's crucifixion, Jesus' followers would carry forward His message, obeying His command: "Go ye therefore, and teach all nations, baptizing them in the name of the Father, and of the Son, and of the Holy Ghost: teaching them to observe all things whatsoever I have commanded you: and, lo, I am with you alway, even unto the end of the world" (Matt. 28:19, 20).

Championing Christ's cause, His followers began their work in what historians now call the *Apostolic Age* (about A.D. 33 to A.D. 100). Spanning the lives of the apostles, it was a period of explosive growth built on the ideals of Christian love that Jesus planted thickly into the hearts of His followers. Peter, Paul, and John grew to be His representative apostles. Jerusalem became the parent church for all Christianity.

However, opposition to Christianity was immediate. An angry mob stoned Stephen, the first Christian martyr, and the persecution of Christ's followers began. Christians would be tortured, humiliated, and sometimes killed for the next 200 years. It has been said that "where God raises up a church, the devil builds a chapel nearby." Soon the apostle Paul had to write to his church members in Galatia to express his dismay over their departure from the faith. "O foolish Galatians, who hath bewitched you, that ye should not obey the truth, before whose eyes Jesus Christ hath been evidently set forth, crucified among you?" (Gal. 3:1).

We know little or nothing about how many Christians there were by the end of the first century. Undoubtedly, the congregations were small and came mainly from the lower classes of society. The New Testament speaks mostly of fishermen, slaves, and common people. Paul says: "Now remember what you were, my brothers, when God called you. From the human point of view few of you were wise or powerful or of high social standing" (1 Cor. 1:26, TEV). Christians met in little groups in private homes. They would not have church buildings until many years later.

The second period of church history was the *Age of the Early Church Fathers* (A.D. 100-A.D. 321). The apostles had passed from the scene, and the generations of church leaders who followed grew more and more distant,

timewise, from Christianity's birth. Persecution
continued off and on, but the courage of the
martyrs and the unjust treatment of the
Christians served only to encourage the spread
of Christianity. Although this era began with
the Christian church as a tiny minority, the
church grew and prospered until it became
officially accepted in the Roman Empire.

In this period the church organized itself
on a more and more sophisticated level. About
the year A.D. 155 a church leader named
Ignatius mentioned the Catholic Church as an
organization in contrast to the catholic church
(small c), which means the universal church.
Actually he was pointing out the difference between the heretics and the true believers, but
the name stuck and was generally adopted by
the end of the century. Many point to this time
as an early recognition of what we know as the
Roman Catholic Church of today.

During the Age of the Early Church
Fathers, the Roman emperor Constantine ended
persecution, legalized Christianity, and made
Sunday the official day of worship in A.D. 321.

Speaking of Christianity's unbelievable tri-
umph, the historian Philip Schaff states:
"Romans, with all their might and policy, could
bring conquered nations only into a mechanical
conglomeration, a giant body without a soul;
Christianity, by purely moral means, founded a
universal spiritual empire and a communion of
saints, which stands unshaken to this day"

(History of the Christian Church, vol. 1, p. 449). Schaff continues: "Christianity reformed society from the bottom, and built upwards until it reached the middle and higher classes, and at last the emperor himself" *(ibid.,* vol. 2, p. 386).

Some estimate that by this time the church may have reached a membership of 10 or 12 million—about one tenth of the population of the Roman Empire. However, there was a downside to such growth: "The Roman state . . . could not be transformed by a magical stroke. The Christianizing of the state amounted therefore in great measure to a paganizing and secularizing of the church. The world overcame the church, as much as the church overcame the world" *(ibid.,* vol. 3, p. 93).

Furthermore, a Roman Catholic Church leader observes of that time: "We are told in various ways by Eusebius, that Constantine, in order to recommend the new religion to the heathen, transferred into it the outward ornaments to which they had been accustomed in their own. It is not necessary to go into a subject which the diligence of Protestant writers has made familiar to most of us. The use of temples, and these dedicated to particular saints, and ornamented on occasions with branches of trees; incense, lamps, and candles; votive offerings on the recovery from illness; holy water; asylums; holy days and seasons, use of calendars, processions, blessings on the fields; sacerdotal vestments, the tonsure, the ring in marriage, turning to the East, images at a later date, perhaps the ecclesiastical chant, and the Kyrie Eleison, are all of pagan origin, and sanctified by their adoption into the church" (Cardinal J. H. Newman, *An Essay on the Development of Christian Doctrine,* pp. 359, 360).

The years from A.D. 311 to A.D. 590 saw the solidification of Catholic beliefs and the cementing of the spheres of church and state. Also, the rise to dominance of the bishop at Rome as pope was formally declared by Pope Gelasius I in A.D. 494. He declared to the patriarchs of Constantinople, Antioch, Alexandria, and Jerusalem that the Roman Church was "over all the others in the world" (Kenneth Latourette, *A History of Christianity,* vol. 1, p. 187). It was during this time that the Roman Empire went into serious decline as a world power.

As the empire's political power faded, a major power shift took place when its administration moved to Constantinople. The Roman Empire divided into two spheres: the east, with headquarters in Constantinople; and the west, with its headquarters in Rome. Thereafter, the church at Rome played an ever-growing political role in the Western Roman Empire. As the imperial power vanished, the ecclesiastical influence grew. By the time of Pope Gregory I (A.D. 590-A.D. 604) the power of the church leadership was, for all practical purposes, absolute.

Historians usually refer to the fourth period of church history as the *Middle Ages* or the *medieval period* (which actually means the middle period between ancient and modern times). Dating from approximately A.D. 590 to A.D. 1517, this period represents the high-water mark of ecclesiastical power.

As the Roman Empire weakened, barbarian tribes invaded the territory and divided the empire into many kingdoms ruled by tribal chiefs. These invasions sharply curtailed trade. Europe became divided into manors, or very large estates, that supplied all the needs for those who lived and worked there. Whole towns were abandoned as their populations moved onto the manors as peasants subject to the landlord. A bishop of the era described the people as "those who pray, those who fight, and those who labor." People had a life span of about 30 years, and fewer than 20 percent traveled more than 10 miles from their birthplace. Typical peasants would live in a crude hut, sleep on a mattress filled with straw, and work the fields of the owner along with a small plot for themselves.

During these dark times the church kept the light of Christianity alive, but just barely. The missionary work of Christ had its effect on the people. The church provided hospitals for the sick and inns for travelers. However, the church also became the largest landholder in Western Europe. Many high-ranking church leaders lived as wealthy and powerful rulers, more like worldly noblemen than humble pastors. The abuse of religious power and position of the church leaders caused a yearning for change in the hearts of many who would later be called the "Reformers" of the church.

From about A.D. 1000 onward, civilization began to reawaken. Eventually people moved back to the towns and cities. Trade commenced again, a middle class of wealthy merchants evolved, and people had more time to devote to culture and learning. Nation states arose in France and England. A religious interest began to stir among the people, led by individuals from within the Roman Catholic Church itself.

One such early Reformer was John Wycliffe (c. 1329-1384), an English priest famous for translating the Bible from Latin into English and for being a doctrinal reformer. Because he translated the Bible into the common language of his people and spoke for sweeping reforms, certain leaders of his church condemned him as a heretic. Forty-four years after his death, Pope Martin V had his bones dug up, burned, and the ashes thrown into a stream as a demonstration of the church's rejection of his work.

Another early Reformer was John Huss (1373-1415), a Czech priest and teacher at the University of Prague, who, as Wycliffe before him, also preached for a reform of the church. He was condemned as a heretic and burned at the stake. The library in Prague has three medallions that represent the relationship of

Wycliffe, Huss, and Martin Luther. The first shows Wycliffe striking sparks on a stone. In the second Huss starts the fire. And the third depicts Luther holding a flaming torch.

Martin Luther (1483-1546), the man holding the torch, was also a priest and university professor. In a way, the next period of church history, the *Protestant Reformation*, lasts from Martin Luther to modern times. Martin Luther said of its beginning: "If you read all the annals of the past, you will find no century like this since the birth of Christ. Such building and planting, such good living and dressing, such enterprise and commerce, such a stir in all the arts, has not been since Christ came into the world. And how numerous are the sharp and intelligent people who leave nothing hidden and unturned: even a boy of twenty years knows more nowadays than was known formerly by twenty doctors of divinity" (quoted in Philip Schaff, *History of the Christian Church*, vol. 7, p. 2).

It should be noted that the Reformers were all baptized, confirmed, and educated in the Roman Catholic Church. It was the abuses of the church that they wanted to reform. Not one of them ever planned to form a new or independent "Protestant" church.

The Reformers pressed their case in three key areas: 1. The teachings of the Bible are always superior to the traditional teachings of the leaders of the church. 2. Faith is better than religious works, that is, attempts to earn salvation through personal effort. 3. A person can pray directly to God without needing a priest to help or act as an intermediary.

Out of these three basic arguments eventually came the formation of the modern Protestant churches. In varying degrees these emphases continue to exist today. Most Protestants still hold with the fundamental teaching of Martin Luther that the Bible and the Bible only is the all-sufficient standard for Christians. Further, they believe that human beings cannot work or buy their way into the kingdom of God. Finally, they hold that one can have direct access to the throne of God without the aid of a priest, saint, or ecclesiastical leader to help the prayers along. As the Scriptures state: "Let us, then, hold firmly to the faith we possess. For we have a great High Priest who has gone into the very presence of God—Jesus, the Son of God" (Heb. 4:14, TEV).

For Further Study

Latourette, Kenneth. "Catholic Name." *A History of Christianity.*

"Middle Ages." *World Book Encyclopedia.*

Schaff, Philip. "A Body Without a Soul." *History of the Christian Church.*

The Mystery Surrounding Jesus' Real Birthday

The Scriptures mention only two birthdays:

that of Pharaoh (Gen. 40:20) and Herod (Matt. 14:6). Some Bible scholars feel that God intentionally omitted the date or even the month of Jesus' birth to discourage worship of a day rather than the worship of our Saviour, Jesus Christ.

One dictionary defines the traditional day of Jesus' birth (Christmas) as: "the festival of the Christian church observed annually on the twenty-fifth day of December, in memory of the birth of Jesus Christ." Please note that the dictionary stated that December 25 was in memory of, not the actual birthday of, Jesus. We have no basis for assigning December 25 as Christ's birthday.

The Scriptures record: "And there were in the same country shepherds abiding in the field, keeping watch over their flock by night" (Luke 2:8). Shepherds stayed with their flocks day and night during most of the year. However, during the cold, rainy winter season they kept their flocks sheltered. Therefore, it would seem most likely that Jesus was born at some other time of the year, since the shepherds were still "abiding" with their flocks.

"The exact dates of Christ's birth, ministry, and death are not precisely known but can be determined with reasonable accuracy. By an error of four or five years in determining the year of Christ's birth, Dionysius Exiguus, a sixth-century Roman abbot, misnumbered the years of his new Christian Era. He placed the birth of Christ at least four or five years too late. . . . Accordingly, His birth may doubtless be assigned to the late fall of 5 B.C. or winter of 5/4 B.C." *(SDA Bible Dictionary,* p. 588).

It never ceases to amaze us that on December 25, people freely give gifts to everyone except the One whose birthday is being celebrated. Observing how many celebrate Christmas today, one can't help seeing the wisdom of God in keeping Jesus' real birthday a secret.

The Bible and the Mystery of Death

What happens when people die? People imagine all kinds of things. Most Christians just assume that at least the good go immediately to heaven. After all, it is a comforting thought. But strangely enough, the Bible says something else. Jesus said that dead people were asleep. And He wasn't alone. The apostle Paul as well as Daniel, a prophet of the Old Testament, said the same thing.

Jesus said: " 'Our friend Lazarus has fallen asleep, but I will go and wake him up.' The disciples answered, 'If he is asleep, Lord, he will get well.' " Although Jesus meant that Lazarus had died, they thought He meant natural sleep. So Jesus told them plainly, "Lazarus is dead" (John 11:11-13, TEV).

As the story of Lazarus' death continues, the man's sister objects to the removal of the stone sealing the grave because of the stench of decomposition from her brother's body. "Martha, the dead man's sister, answered, 'There will be a bad smell, Lord. He has been buried four days!'" (verse 39, TEV).

As the narrative continues, Jesus does raise the man from death to life. Friends release him from his grave wrappings and set him free. One wonders how Lazarus would have felt, if he had already spent four days in heaven, to have to return to the sin-filled earth and eventually have to face death all over again.

The apostle Paul said: "But I would not have you to be ignorant, brethren, concerning them which are asleep, that ye sorrow not, even as others which have no hope" (1 Thess. 4:13). Furthermore, Daniel offered the same thought when he said: "And many of them that sleep in the dust of the earth shall awake" (Dan. 12:2).

Were these inspired individuals wrong about what happens to us at death? Actually, they were only repeating what the rest of the Bible has to say about death.

For instance, according to Psalm 146:4, when someone dies, "his breath goeth forth, he returneth to his earth; in that very day his thoughts perish." In addition, Scripture says: "For the living know that they shall die: but the dead know not any thing" (Eccl. 9:5). Verse 6 adds: "Also their love, and their hatred, and their envy, is now perished; neither have they any more a portion for ever in any thing that is done under the sun."

Moreover, consider Psalm 17:15: "As for me, I will behold thy face in righteousness: I shall be satisfied, when I awake, with thy likeness." First Thessalonians 4:16 declares: "For the Lord himself shall descend from heaven with a shout, with the voice of the archangel, and with the trump of God: and the dead in Christ shall rise first."

In summary, perhaps the easiest way to make sense of these texts is to compare death and resurrection to our experience of having a good night's sleep. We fall asleep and become totally unaware of what is going on around us. In other parts of the world wars can rage, volcanoes erupt, and floods destroy while we sleep soundly on, undisturbed. It is not until the morning, when we awaken, that we become aware of what has happened.

Jesus says it's like that when we die—we are as asleep, awaiting the resurrection. That is true of both the bad and the good alike. The Bible says that a day is coming when some will be resurrected to damnation and others to eternal life. When Jesus returns to earth for the final time, all the wicked who have ever lived will be judged and will receive their just reward (Rev. 20:11-15).

One day each of us will go the way of all flesh and die, and as Jesus said, we will sleep until He calls us from our graves with the sound of the trumpet and the voice of the archangel.

Paul and the Slave

Xenia, Ohio, this author's birthplace, has been noted for two things: the disastrous tornadoes of 1974, and as a site of an organization called the Underground Railroad. This railroad that was neither underground nor had any tracks was really part of a system to help slaves escape to freedom in the middle 1800s. Today Xenians are duly proud of their forebears for having done their part to help rescue their fellow human beings from the cruel oppression of slavery.

Oddly, the apostle Paul also had an opportunity to assist a runaway slave. However, instead of aiding him to escape, Paul sent him back! The little New Testament book of Philemon is a personal letter he wrote on behalf of the runway slave Onesimus. The apostle addressed it to Philemon, the slave's owner. The letter does not explain the how or why of Onesimus' escape. All we have today is a copy of the letter to the Christian slave owner.

Slavery was widespread in the Roman Empire. Scholars estimate that at times slaves comprised more than half of the population. Because there were so many slaves, the ruling classes made severe laws to keep order. The master had absolute power of life and death over his slaves. The punishment for running away could be death by crucifixion.

According to the Roman law, slaves "had no head in the state, no name, no title, or register;

they were not capable of being injured; nor could they take by purchase or descent; they had no heirs, and therefore could make no will; they were not entitled to the rights and considerations of matrimony, and therefore had no relief in case of adultery; . . . they could be sold, transferred, or pawned, as goods or personal estate, . . . they might be tortured for evidence, punished at the discretion of their lord, and even put to death by his authority" (Philip Schaff, *History of the Christian Church,* vol. 1, p. 447).

Moreover, it is important to note that a slave could have been a highly educated person brought to Rome from some distant conquest. Often teachers, philosophers, and physicians might be slaves. However, slaves had the possibility of being freed. If properly released, they could assume positions of responsibility within the empire.

The Acts of the Apostles, by Ellen G. White, makes the following comments about Paul's decision to send the slave back to his master: "It was not the apostle's work to overturn arbitrarily or suddenly the established order of society. To attempt this would be to prevent the success of the gospel. But he taught principles which struck at the very foundation of slavery and which, if carried into effect, would surely undermine the whole system. 'Where the Spirit of the Lord is, there is liberty,' he declared (2 Cor. 3:17). When converted, the slave became a member of the body of Christ, and as such was to be loved and treated as a brother, a fel-

low heir with his master to the blessings of God
and the privileges of the gospel. On the other
hand, servants were to perform their duties,
'not with eyeservice, as men pleasers; but as
the servants of Christ, doing the will of God
from the heart' (Eph. 6:6)" (pp. 459, 460).

Unlike the Underground Railroad, which
could help a slave gain freedom for this lifetime
in Canada, Paul sent the slave back with the as-
surance of freedom for eternity in Christ Jesus.
Even so, it must have been an extremely hard
choice to urge a fellow human to return volun-
tarily to slavery, however temporary it might be.

For Further Study

Lewis, Naphtali, and Meyer Reinhold. "The Landed Estate."
    Roman Civilization. Sourcebook I: The Republic. New York:
    Harper and Row, 1966.
Schaff, Philip. *History of the Christian Church.* Vol. 1, p. 445.
"Slavery." *Encyclopaedia Britannica.*

Unusual Things in the Bible

Moses With Horns

"And Aaron and the children of Israel
seeing the face of Moses horned, were afraid
to come near" (Ex. 34:30, Douay). This
unfortunate mistranslation led artists such as
Michelangelo to create a Moses with horns
sticking out of his head. The statue, located
in the Church of Saint Peter in Chains

in Rome, is one example of where the mis-translation led.

The Rule of the Gleaners

"And when ye reap the harvest of your land, thou shalt not wholly reap the corners of thy field, neither shalt thou gather the gleanings of thy harvest. And thou shalt not glean thy vineyard, neither shalt thou gather every grape of thy vineyard; thou shalt leave them for the poor and stranger: I am the Lord your God" (Lev. 19:9, 10). A similar practice of leaving a little behind also applied to the olive grove. This act of charity required that needy persons still had to work for what they received, leaving them with their dignity.

A Man Should Not Shave His Beard?

"Ye shall not round the corners of your heads, neither shalt thou mar the corners of thy beard" (verse 27). The Jews considered their beards as a sign of manhood. Some scholars have suggested that some surrounding religions cut off part of the beard as an offering to pagan gods. Others read into this text the idea that no man should shave his beard. This would be a problem for American Indians and others with little or no facial hair. It underscores the absurdity of misusing the Bible.

No Tattoos?

"You shall not . . . print any marks upon you: I am the Lord" (verse 28). The passage probably refers to tattooing or branding of the flesh. Members of a number of ancient religions would mark or scarify their skin in honor of their deities. God wanted His people to avoid any practice that would cause them to identify with a false religion.

Hollow of the Thigh

When we stand, an indention forms on the side of the hip. A passage in Scripture alludes to this. Genesis 32:25 says: "And when he [the angel of the Lord] saw that he prevailed not against him, he touched the hollow of his thigh; and the hollow of Jacob's thigh was out of joint, as he wrestled with him."

From this arose a Jewish tradition. Verse 32 tells us that "the children of Israel eat not of the sinew which shrank, which is upon the hollow of the thigh, unto this day: because he touched the hollow of Jacob's thigh in the sinew that shrank."

The Hebrew word translated "shrank" is not clear. Perhaps it could be rendered "hip," with the passage reading "the sinew of the hip." As a result, some Jews refrain from eating the Achilles tendon of animals used for food, but how this part of Jacob's anatomy came to be identified as the sinew that shrank is uncertain.

Adam's Rib

Popular tradition says that a man has one less rib than a woman because God removed it to create Eve. The Bible says: "And the Lord God caused a deep sleep to fall upon Adam, and he slept: and he took one of his ribs, and closed up the flesh instead thereof; and the rib, which the Lord God had taken from man, made he a woman, and brought her unto the man" (Gen. 2:21, 22).

As in the case of many traditions, this one is based on a true event, but the tradition itself is untrue. Although an occasional rare person is born with 11 pairs of ribs, the overwhelming majority of all people, male and female, are born with 12 pairs of ribs. Contrary to popular belief, men and women have exactly the same number of ribs. The biblical event was true, but the folklore about men and women having different numbers of ribs is false.

Phylacteries and Mezuzahs

Jesus said of the scribes and Pharisees: "They do everything so that people will see them. Look at the straps [phylacteries] with scripture verses on them which they wear on their foreheads and arms, and notice how large they are!" (Matt. 23:5, TEV). In Jesus' time every male Israelite above the age of 13 was required to put on a head and hand phylactery at daily morning prayer. Some Orthodox Jews still do this today. They wear small black leather boxes containing passages of Scripture tied with a leather thong in the center of the forehead and on the left arm above the elbow.

The whole idea of wearing the phylactery rests on a literal interpretation of Deuteronomy

6:4-9, which reads: "Israel, remember this! The Lord—and the Lord alone—is our God. Love the Lord your God with all your heart, with all your soul, and with all your strength. Never forget these commands that I am giving you today. Teach them to your children. Repeat them when you are at home and when you are away, when you are resting and when you are working. Tie them on your arms and wear them on your foreheads as a reminder. Write them on the doorposts of your houses and on your gates" (TEV).

The final sentence of the passage above refers to writing Scripture on the doorposts of houses. Many Jews still attempt to do this. Both Jewish homes and public places have a small ornate container, called a Mezuzah, attached to the right doorpost, that contains a small scroll with the words from Deuteronomy 4:4-9 and 11:13-21. Most of the objects are about the size of a felt-tip pen. They can be beautifully made of silver and gold or be just plain and simple. The standard ritual is to rub your hand over the Mezuzah as you leave the building.

The Book of Esther

This Old Testament book does not mention the name of God. However, a twelfth-century rabbi declared the book of Esther second in importance and value only to the Law of Moses, the Pentateuch, or first five books of the Hebrew Scriptures. Hitler so hated the book of Esther that he banned the annual Jewish festival of Purim. The festival celebrated the deeds of the book's main character in her battle to save the Jewish people.

Why Many Bible Words Are in Italics

We wish that every book of the Bible were a model of correct grammar, punctuation, syntax, and high literary style. However, the Bible is a distinctive collection of small books and letters written by a range of authors that includes prophets, fishermen, kings, a lawyer, priests, a doctor, and even a tax collector. In addition to the wide variety of the language skills of the authors, many of the old manuscripts have missing letters and words because of copying errors.

Also, translators face the challenge of duplicating the exact meaning of words in other languages. To meet these difficulties, the translators carefully add words to the text and put them in italics to alert the reader that they have added the word.

They insert the italicized words for two reasons. Some of the words in italics may not have any equivalents in the Hebrew or Greek text. The translators supply them to make the meaning of the sentence more understandable or in order to make the passage read more smoothly in English. For instance, in Matthew 5:3-10 the word *are* has been added to smooth the reading. The texts all read "Blessed *are* . . ." with the supplied word *are* in italics.

Another example of how words have been supplied occurs in John 5:2: "Now there is at Jerusalem by the sheep *market* a pool, which is called in the Hebrew tongue Bethesda, having five porches." The Greek actually says "by the sheep a pool." The reader can quickly see that common sense calls for the word *market* to make the passage more understandable.

The Geneva Bible of 1577 first used italics in this fashion.

Why People Are Baptized at the Leaning Tower of Pisa

John the Baptist did not invent the practice of baptism. The Scriptures clearly indicate that it was already in existence when Jesus asked John to perform the baptismal rite on Him. Matthew 3:14 tells how John the Baptist is surprised that Jesus would ask for baptism. Astonished at His request, John tells Him that it is he who should receive the baptism. However, Jesus insists, and John baptizes Him.

Converts to Judaism were baptized to wash away the impurities of heathenism. They were baptized by complete immersion in running water.

The Scriptures say: "And John also was baptizing in Aenon near to Salim, because there

was much water there" (John 3:23). A fresco
(painting with water colors on wet plaster) in
the catacombs is the earliest known depiction of
the baptism of Jesus. The picture depicts John
the Baptist giving Jesus a helping hand as He
steps up out of the water. In this second-cen-
tury fresco, John the Baptist has short hair and
no beard, and Jesus may have collar-length
hair and a short beard.

Baptism in the Christian church began
with the practice of total immersion. The early
Christians continued to follow the example of
Jesus until the church began to modify the
practice because of the lack of water in desert
countries and because of other problems.
Examples of early baptistries are plentiful.
One of the more famous examples is in a building on the grounds of the Leaning Tower of
Pisa. At Pisa, Italy, three structures were built
on a square named the Piassa dei Miracoli.
They are the famous leaning bell tower, the
cathedral, and beside them, a separate building
containing a baptistry and altar. Round and ornate in the style of the leaning tower, it has a
large dome-shaped roof. The building's only
purpose is to house a large baptismal pool.

Baptistries such as the one at Pisa were built
separate from the church because baptisms were
conducted infrequently. Therefore, when baptisms were carried out, hundreds of people
would be baptized at one time. Over the years it
became easier simply to pour a little water over

the candidate or even sprinkle a few drops (called affusion) upon them. However, the change has no scriptural authority. It was a human idea. Roman Catholic cardinal James Gibbons says: "For several centuries after the establishment of Christianity baptism was usually conferred by immersion; but since the twelfth century the practice of baptizing by infusion has prevailed in the Catholic Church, as this manner is attended with less inconvenience than baptism by immersion" (*Faith of Our Fathers*, p. 228).

But the example of Jesus still stands as the only baptism demonstrated in the Bible. The Bible doesn't say that John sprinkled anyone in the wilderness. Instead, it declares: "John did baptize in the wilderness" (Mark 1:4). Paul says of baptism: "By our baptism, then, we were buried with him and shared his death, in order that, just as Christ was raised from death by the glorious power of the Father, so also we might live a new life" (Rom. 6:4, TEV). One doesn't bury a body by tossing a little dust on it. The symbolism is still the same today as it was during the times of Jesus. Baptism by total immersion symbolizes the death of the old self, the washing away of sin, and the beginning of a new life in Christ Jesus.

For Further Study

"Baptism." *World Book Encyclopedia.*

Brown, Henry F. "Baptisteries." *Baptism Through the Centuries.* P. 3.

Schaff, Philip. *History of the Christian Church.*

Don't Confuse Us With Them

Although at first highly respected by the
Roman Empire, in time the Jews acquired a more
negative reputation. They despised the Romans'
many pagan gods because of religious reasons and
fought against Roman occupation of Palestine.
After they repeatedly rebelled against their heavy-
handed Roman rulers, many looked upon the Jews
as a constant source of trouble for the empire.

This negative image of Jews spilled over into
the early Christian community. Christianity
arose within Judaism, and at first Christians
considered themselves Jews who accepted
Jesus as the promised Jewish Messiah. Only
gradually did Christians see themselves as dis-
tinct from the rest of the Jews. The conversion
of non-Jews made the church increasingly non-
Jewish in makeup. But Christians and Jews still
held many things in common. Since Christians
and Jews both kept Saturday as Sabbath, many
Romans looked upon Christians as nothing more
than a Jewish cult. For the Sabbathkeeping
Christians it was a case of being in the right place
but at the wrong time. Although they were not
interested in overthrowing the government, as
were many Jews, the Romans looked upon them
as one and the same.

So in response to their mistaken Jewish
identity, the early Christians began to emphasize worship on a separate day from the Jews,
to set themselves apart. They soon began hav-

ing their church meetings on Sunday, which was already a Roman sacred day. Further, in order to justify their Sunday worship, the early Christians stressed that the new day of worship was in honor of the resurrection of Jesus.

Finally in A.D. 321, after Christians rose to be a powerful force, the Roman state officially recognized the civil day of rest as Sunday, the formerly pagan day dedicated to the worship of the sun. The law read: "On the venerable Day of the Sun let the magistrates and people residing in cities rest, and let all workshops be closed. In the country, however, persons engaged in agriculture may freely and lawfully continue their pursuits; because it often happens that another day is not so suitable for grain-sowing or for vine-planting; lest by neglecting the proper moment for such operations the bounty of heaven should be lost."

Today many still honor the Day of the Sun as their official worship day, not knowing that Sunday observance crept into the church partly from a Christian desire to avoid being confused with a rebellious minority.

For Further Study

Bacchiocchi, Samuele. *From Sabbath to Sunday: A Historical Investigation of the Rise of Sunday Observance in Early Christianity*. Rome: Pontifical Gregorian University Press, 1977.

Schaff, Philip. "The Lord's Day." *History of the Christian Church*.

The Mystery Revealed of How to Live Forever

No one wants to die! God has planted a strong desire in each of us to live. We all by nature want to be immortal and exist forever. But in the sinful state into which we were born — and didn't ask for — we are subject to death. We are mortal. The Bible has much to say about the human desire to live forever and what to do about it. And unlike the sensational claims about finding the secret of eternal life that you read while waiting in the grocery store checkout lines, what the Bible says is true.

The apostle Paul wrote a letter of encouragement to his church members in Corinth about immortality: "Behold, I shew you a mystery; We shall not all sleep, but we shall all be changed, in a moment, in the twinkling of an eye, at the last trump: for the trumpet shall sound, and the dead shall be raised incorruptible, and we shall be changed. For this corruptible must put on incorruption, and this mortal must put on immortality. . . . O death, where is thy sting? O grave, where is thy victory?" (1 Cor. 15:51-55).

The point Paul is making is obvious: we do not now have immortality. The apostle knew this because of an event that happened back in the Garden of Eden with Adam and Eve. In Genesis 3:4, 5 we read: "And the serpent said unto the woman, Ye shall not surely die: for God doth know that in the day ye eat thereof, then your eyes shall be opened, and ye shall be as gods, knowing good and evil." Here in the familiar story of the temptation and fall of Adam and Eve, Satan speaks through the serpent and says that the human couple will not die, but that they will just change their state and be as gods.

Indeed, Satan's lie was correct in part. They did learn firsthand what evil was, yet even though Satan told them otherwise, they still died. The process of being made alive was reversed, and they perished. In Genesis 2:7 we read of their creation: "And the Lord God formed man of the dust of the ground, and breathed into his nostrils the breath of life; and man became a living soul." It is interesting to note that a human being is a combination of two things. First, the elements of earth, physical matter; and second, the spark of life, or the spirit of life—something that only God can give. These two things combine together, and a human being becomes a living being.

This mysterious spark of life, the spirit of life, is something that has eluded the understanding of our greatest scientific minds. They cannot figure out what makes something turn from inanimate to animate, from dead matter to living matter. Furthermore, when we die and the living process reverses, the Bible says: "Then shall the dust return to the earth as it was: and the spirit shall return unto God who gave it" (Eccl. 12:7). Psalm 146:4 echoes this thought:

"His breath goeth forth, he returneth to his earth; in that very day his thoughts perish."

At the time of death we, like those who have gone before, sleep and await the return of our Lord. However, Paul gives us encouragement: "For as in Adam all die, even so in Christ shall all be made alive. But every man in his own order: Christ the firstfruits; afterward they that are Christ's at his coming" (1 Cor. 15:22, 23).

The Mystery of the Number 666

There is only one number in the whole Bible that inspiration declares to be symbolic. Revelation 13:18 says of 666: "Here is wisdom. Let him that hath understanding count the number of the beast: for it is the number of a man; and his number is Six hundred threescore and six."

One of the methods scholars have used to try to unlock the meaning of the number and determine the identity of the mystery man is an ancient Greek idea called Gematria. This technique seeks to find a hidden meaning in a name or word by assigning a numerical value to each letter in the word. Countless authors have tried to use this method to identify the person John labels 666, but all have come short in absolutely pinning down, once and for all, who this mystery man is.

One of the earliest to speculate on the being was the early church scholar Irenaeus

(c. A.D. 130-A.D. 202), who identified the beast as the antichrist. Yet he was cautious and said of his suggested list of names: "It is therefore more certain, and less hazardous, to await the fulfillment of the prophecy, than to be making surmise, and casting about for any names that may present themselves, inasmuch as many names can be found possessing the number mentioned."

But people would not give up trying. Gematria has been used to find a numerical value of 666 for such names as Nero, Napoleon, John Knox, Hitler, Lateinos (which means the Roman Empire), Henry Kissinger, and on and on.

During the Reformation (about A.D. 1500) some proposed that 666 stood for *Vicarious Filii Dei*, meaning "vicar of the Son of God," one of the titles of the pope of Rome. Using Latin numerals, it is:

V =	5	F =	. . .	D =	500
I =	1	I =	1	E =	. . .
C =	100	L =	50	I =	1
A =	. . .	I =	1		
R =	. . .	I =	1		
I =	1				
U =	5				
S =	. . .				

$$\overline{112} \ + \ \overline{53} \ + \ \overline{501} \ = \ 666 \text{ total}$$

However, Catholic scholars, put off by

such speculation about their church leader, turned the tables and used the same method on their accuser, Martin Luther. It seems his name can also be made to add up to 666.

One wonders why John the revelator could have not been more specific. Some have suggested that he really wanted to identify the Roman emperor as the beast, but had to hide the true meaning in case his writings fell into the hands of his enemies. John was living during a time of Christian persecution and was probably serving a prison sentence on the Isle of Patmos for his beliefs. A direct attack against the emperor would have been treason and certain death. It is therefore suggested that he coded the name of the emperor into a number that those who heard it would understand. However, we who read the passage some 1,900 years later find it impossible to put John's code in reverse and, with total certainty, determine the exact name he intended.

Moreover, many people see a dual meaning in this passage. They see Revelation 13 as a message to the churches of John's time, and also a prophetic message for times to come.

For Further Study

Schaff, Philip. *History of the Christian Church*. Vol. 1, pp. 841-853.

Can Bible Numbers Be Dangerous?

It's not the way the Bible uses numbers that makes them weird. It's what people do with the numbers that makes them say strange things. Actually, the Bible writers most often used numbers in a normal fashion to simply count things, such as a military census, population statistics, etc. However, sometimes they employed numbers in a symbolic way to represent things such as the mysterious man of Revelation 13:18. Additionally, some feel that the numbers found in the Bible can be used in mystical ways that have secret religious meanings.

First, consider the symbolic use of the number 7. The number 7 occurs in nearly 600 passages of the Bible. Many people feel, basing their belief on selected Bible texts, that 7 is a number symbolic of completeness. For instance, God finished the Creation in six days and rested on the seventh. This, the beginning of the seven-day weekly cycle, seems to be at the root of the abundant use of the number 7 in the Scriptures.

Seven appears throughout the Bible. In the Old Testament a prophet told Naaman to dip in the Jordan seven times in order to cure his leprosy (2 Kings 5:10). Obviously, God could have healed Naaman after any number of times, but He had the prophet instruct Naaman to immerse himself seven times as a symbolic act of faith. Likewise, in the New Testament the number 7 appears symbolically in the message to the seven churches (Rev. 1:11). In this case, while we know that there were many more than seven churches, the use of 7 is symbolic, indicating completeness in that God intended the message for all of the churches of that area.

Indeed, although the Bible employs numbers in a variety of interesting ways, we must always interpret them by the way the Bible writer used the number or by its setting. However, this cannot be said of mystical numbers. Imagination, speculation, and plain old guessing make up large parts of the mystical definitions of numbers. A person should carefully consider what one is told a number means or stands for before accepting the idea as truth.

Numbers are like statistics—if you manipulate them enough, they will tell you almost anything you want. For example, some say the number 1 is the number of God, while the number 2 means division or separation. However, another says the number 1 means unity and the number 2 means discord and death. Who is right? Maybe neither one! But scholars think we know who started all the confusion with numbers—his name was Pythagoras.

As far as scholars can tell, this whole idea of numerology got a big boost around the sixth century B.C. when an ancient philosopher named Pythagoras developed the idea that all things can be expressed in numbers because everything in the universe can ultimately be reduced to a series of numbers. Pythagoras and his followers gave divine significance to most of the numbers up to 50. They considered even numbers to be feminine and odd masculine. He mystically associated numbers with colors, virtues, and many other things.

Pythagoras was not alone in his fascination with numbers. The Babylonians, Egyptians, and Aramaeans seem to have used mystical numbers earlier, but it was Pythagoras who created a highly organized system. His thoughts spread to Italy from Greece and then eventually to the Bible land of Palestine. The influence of Pythagoras' number systems shows up in the nonbiblical writings called the Apocrypha and in the writings of the Gnostics (a split-off group of Christians during the early centuries of the church).

The teachings of Pythagoras saw a rapid growth in influence when the early Christian church leader Augustine (died A.D. 430) showed an intense interest in numerology. Later, numerology spread to the Jews and was featured in a category of their writings called cabalistic literature. The cabalists taught that there was a deeper meaning to the names, words, and letters of the Bible, and that one could find hidden mysteries about the divine through them. Interest in numerology continues today.

Thoughtful people must wonder that if God wanted the gospel of Jesus Christ to go to all the world, why would He then hide any knowledge? Why would the Holy Scriptures, formed by the inspiration of God, contain secret information? Why would someone have to have some special knowledge or wisdom to understand the Bible? The apostle Paul wrote to the young Timothy and instructed him: "Study to shew thyself approved unto God, a workman that needeth not to be ashamed, rightly dividing the word of truth" (2 Tim. 2:15). Paul did not tell him to "speculate" to show himself approved.

Bible students should accept the Scriptures for what they say at face value and follow the thoughts of the English philosopher William of Ockham, who said, "Consider the simplest version as the most probable."

For Further Study

Ackroyd, Peter R., and Christopher F. Evans, eds. *Cambridge History of the Bible.* Vol. 1, pp. 559, 560.

Davis, John J. *Biblical Numerology.* Grand Rapids: Baker Book House, 1968.

To Eat . . . or Not to Eat?

Orthodox Jews are selective about what they eat because of ancient dietary advice God gave in the Bible. He instructed His people as to what was clean and unclean food in Leviticus 11. Basically, the instructions are that clean land animals must chew the cud and have split hooves, and that fish are to have fins and scales. Concerning pork, it states: "Of their flesh shall ye not eat, and their carcase shall ye not touch; they are unclean to you" (Lev. 11:8).

God invented the categories of clean and unclean. He also created all the peoples of the planet, making them physiologically similar. It follows that what is healthy for one person must also have the similar benefits for another. As modern science increases our understanding of the effects of diet and nutrition, we are coming to realize more and more that a healthy diet makes healthy people.

Today many people, for reasons of health, have also chosen to move far beyond the biblical categories of clean and unclean meats to vegetarianism. Others, for spiritual reasons, cite the words of the apostle Paul in 1 Corinthians 6:19, 20: "What? know ye not that your body is the temple of the Holy Ghost which is in you, which ye have of God, and ye are not your own? For ye are bought with a price: therefore glorify God in your body, and in your spirit, which are God's."

Of all of the pros and cons about what exactly is the best diet, this we can know — God said in Psalm 84:11: "No good thing will he withhold from them that walk uprightly." Further, one should note the original human diet described in Genesis 1:29: "I have provided all kinds of grain and all kinds of fruit for you to eat" (TEV).

Why Jesus Went to Church on Saturday

Jesus went to church on what we today call Saturday, as did all the other Jews of His time. He did this because Saturday, the seventh day of the week, is the Sabbath that He formed at the creation of our planet.

If the idea of Jesus the Creator is new to the reader, please consider that the book of Hebrews presents the theme of Christ as Creator. "God . . . hath in these last days spoken unto us by his Son, . . . by whom also he made the worlds" (Heb. 1:1, 2).

As we saw elsewhere, Creation week set the pattern for today's week. "For in six days the Lord made heaven and earth, the sea, and all that in them is, and rested the seventh day: wherefore the Lord blessed the sabbath day, and hallowed it" (Ex. 20:11). God set aside the seventh day of the week as the day on which we should worship Him.

Jesus followed the pattern He established at Creation. He continued to observe the Saturday Sabbath as the divinely appointed time for corporate worship. "As his custom was, he went into the synagogue on the sabbath day, and stood up for to read" (Luke 4:16). Please note that Jesus was on a mission prophesied in Isaiah 42:21. Scripture predicts of Him who was to come that "he will magnify the law, and make it honourable."

"In nothing, perhaps, was this more strik-

ingly fulfilled than in the matter of Sabbath
observance. By their numerous traditional reg-
ulations and senseless restrictions the Jews had
made the Sabbath a burden, and anything but a
delight. Christ removed all these, and by His
life and teachings restored the Sabbath to its
proper place as a day of worship, of contempla-
tion of God, a day for doing acts of charity and
mercy. Thus He magnified it and made it hon-
orable. One of the most prominent features of
Christ's ministry was this work of *Sabbath reform*. Christ did not *abolish* or *change* the
Sabbath; but He did rescue it from the rubbish
of tradition, false ideas, and superstitions by
which it had been degraded. The Pharisees had
placed the institution *above* man, and *against*
man. Christ reversed the order, and said, 'The
sabbath was made *for man,* and not man *for the
sabbath.*' He showed that it was to minister to
the happiness and well-being of both man and
beast" *(Bible Readings for the Home,* p. 426).

The Bible and the Mystery of God's Day

Some things are more important than others. We do not find instructions in the Bible,
for example, that tell us whether to button our
coats from the top down or the bottom up.
Likewise, we do not find a rule that we must
double-knot our tennis shoes when we tie

them. Obviously God gave us intelligence to figure out things like that on our own. However, when God wanted to make a point absolutely clear, He wrote it down Himself. Such is the case with the Ten Commandments. God was so concerned that these 10 guiding principles for all humanity be clearly communicated that He wrote them down with His own finger on tables of stone. "And he gave unto Moses, when he had made an end of communing with him upon mount Sinai, two tables of testimony, tables of stone, written with the finger of God" (Ex. 31:18).

God cared enough to make sure the Ten Commandments were recorded exactly the way He intended. However, not everyone seems to care as much as God did. The matter of obeying all of the Ten Commandments is one of those issues that many people say does not really matter. They argue that "it's just a matter of opinion." Are they right?

We all know that life is not just a simple black-and-white photograph. Life contains many shades of color and hue. We do not all see things exactly alike. Many factors determine why we view things differently. For instance, suppose that two cars bumped into each other in a supermarket parking lot. Almost everyone will agree that three different people can witness such an accident and come up with three different opinions of what happened. Because of this confusion, it has even been suggested that in extreme cases the witnesses should be hypnotized and asked to recall what they really saw. Of course, the idea is that the real truth will be discovered when the person reels off what his or her brain literally recorded. But that is not necessarily so!

Experts tell us that we do not have video cameras in our brains. In other words, what we see, or think we see, comes through our own set of individual experiences and is stored that way in our brains. For instance, the noise of the screeching tires might have caused witnesses to put their hands over their ears. Or the sight of cars about to collide may have caused them to turn their head or jump back and momentarily look away. Naturally, anything that would distract one's attention would tend to distort one's understanding of what really happened. Furthermore, one of the witnesses may have been previously involved in a terrible auto accident and mentally blocked out part of the collision or interpreted the accident within the traumatic framework of his or her own frightening experience.

After the crash, one witness may see a wrecked Corvette, while another sees a red sports car. The third observer may mistake its color for green or gray because of colorblindness. In this example it is easy to understand how three persons could witness an auto mishap and come up with differing opinions of what happened.

However, what about other situations in which people see exactly the same thing? Can people read words printed in black and white and come away with very different opinions of what those words meant? Of course they can. It happens all of the time, especially if they are reading the Bible.

Our Bibles seem to provide much fertile ground for disagreements over what the authors really intended to say. Take, for example, a text found in the Bible that says, "I was in the Spirit on the Lord's day" (Rev. 1:10). Many people interpret the text to mean that Sunday is the Lord's day. Those who feel that John was having his vision on Sunday say that it proves that the apostle worshiped on Sunday and was setting an example for the rest of Christianity.

While it may be true that this event might have happened on Sunday, one has to wonder if it could not have occurred on some other day. Consider again the car accident in the parking lot. Could we say definitely that it took place on a Sunday because the people in one of the cars were dressed up as if for church? And what if we discovered they had a Bible between them on the seat? Would that prove they were going to Sunday school? Or might we find out that the couple were really a minister and his wife on their way to a Thursday morning home visitation?

Sometimes even the brightest and best scholars can read a passage in the Bible and leave with conflicting ideas as to its true meaning. Such is the case with Revelation 1:10. Listed here are the opinions of six noted scholars. We find they do not necessarily agree as to whether the phrase "the Lord's day" refers to Sunday or not. In their various commentaries they say:

Barclay (Westminster Press): "It is quite certain . . ."

Boring (John Knox Press): "It most likely refers to Sunday . . ."

Leon Morris (Tyndale): ". . . the first reference to Christian Sunday."

Phillips (Loizeaux Bros.): "Scholars differ over the expression . . ."

Walvoord (Moody): "There is no solid evidence . . ."

J. Massyngberde Ford *(Anchor Bible)*: "It is very difficult to determine which is meant."

Is it really an important issue whether scholars agree or disagree about the meaning of one solitary text? It depends. Some would say it is like the auto accident. Nobody got hurt, the damage appeared to be very minor, and all of the drivers agreed to settle up immediately on the spot. Those who reason this way say the incident should simply be forgotten. It was not important.

However, what if there was hidden harm? Damage that was not obvious to the untrained eye? Something unexpected? Such might be a reason for reconsidering the meaning of Revelation 1:10. What if someone said his or her interpretation absolutely proves that the apostle John kept Sunday sacred in place of the Sabbath of the Ten Commandments? He or she reasons that by John's example we can say with certainty that the apostle and others transferred Sabbath worship to Sunday.

Those who disagree with this view read Revelation 1:10 and reply that the evidence is simply too meager to draw such a definite conclusion. They think that holding such a strong position oversteps the available facts. Furthermore, they ask, should there not be more evidence presented than just one sentence in the book of Revelation?

By now some readers have to be asking what all the fuss is about. What does it really matter whether the apostle John had a vision on Sunday, Tuesday, or any other day? Indeed, it may not be of crucial importance what day John was in the Spirit. All we can say for sure is that he describes a panoramic vision of the world as it will be in the end-times and a vision of the world to come. Anything beyond that is really speculation.

However, it is not just John's book of Revelation over which the scholars disagree. They cite other places in the Bible that they say also suggests transfer of worship from Saturday to Sunday. Some of those are listed below and are all important events thought to have transpired on Sunday.

◆ Jesus arose from the grave on Sunday. "Now when Jesus was risen early the first day

of the week, he appeared first to Mary
Magdalene, out of whom he had cast seven
devils" (Mark 16:9).

◆ On Sunday Jesus first met with His disciples after His death. "And they, when they
had heard that he was alive, and had been seen
of her, believed not" (verse 11).

◆ On Sunday Jesus imparted the Holy Spirit.
"Receive ye the Holy Ghost" (John 20:22).

◆ On Sunday He commissioned the disciples to preach to all the world. "Go ye into all
the world, and preach the gospel to every crea-
ture" (Mark 16:15).

◆ John is supposed to have received his
revelation on Sunday.

May we return to the two-car accident in
the parking lot analogy? Again, it is a matter of
the witnesses and how they see things. For instance, if every fender-bender known to a witness happened on Sunday, could he or she
therefore speculate that such things happen
only on Sunday? Certainly it is a point to consider and then wisely reject. Reject because we
simply lack enough information to draw a firm
conclusion. After all, the witness might find out
later that studies had shown that most acci-
dents actually happened on Saturday night.

In considering the so-called Sunday events
mentioned in the Scriptures, one is forced to
admit that there just is not a clear "Thus saith
the Lord" in the Bible to indicate any possible
transfer of sanctity from the Sabbath to

Sunday. In fact, the word *Sunday* does not appear in the Bible. Scripture simply refers to what we know as Sunday as the first day of the week. Actually, God gave a name to only one day in the Bible—the Sabbath of the Ten Commandments. Moreover, He blessed and set aside only one day for a holy purpose. We read of it in Genesis 2:3: "And God blessed the seventh day, and sanctified it: because that in it he had rested from all his work which God created and made.", God blessed and sanctified only the Sabbath.

However, some claim that they have actually transferred Sabbath sanctity to Sunday. *The Converts Catechism of Catholic Doctrine* (p. 50), by Peter Geirermann, observes:

"Question: *Why do we observe Sunday instead of Saturday?*

"Answer: We observe Sunday instead of Saturday because the Catholic Church transferred the solemnity from Saturday to Sunday.

"Question: *Why did the Catholic Church substitute Sunday for Saturday?*

"Answer: The church substituted Sunday for Saturday because Christ rose from the dead on Sunday, and the Holy Ghost descended upon the apostles on a Sunday.

"Question: *By what authority did the church substitute Sunday for Saturday?*

"Answer: The church substituted Sunday for Saturday by the plentitude of that divine power which Jesus Christ bestowed upon her."

In *A Doctrinal Catechism* (p. 174), Stephen Keenan asks: *"Have you any other way of proving that the church has power to institute festivals of precept?"* "Had she not such power," he answers, "she could not have done that in which all modern religionists agree with her—she could not have substituted the observance of Sunday, the first day of the week, for the observance of Saturday, the seventh day, a change for which there is no scriptural authority."

An important matter here is who really shifted the sanctity of the Sabbath to Sunday? If we look into the Holy Bible and let it speak for itself, the answer is quite clear. Neither early Christians, Catholics, nor Protestants transferred God's holiness from one day to another. The Sabbath day remains as He created it, because only God can bless and sanctify a day. Human beings may for all sorts of reasons claim to have transferred the solemnity from one day to another, but only the Creator can change what He created. The Scriptures record no such change of mind on God's part. Instead, Jesus says: "Think not that I am come to destroy the law, or the prophets: I am not come to destroy, but to fulfill. For verily I say unto you, Till heaven and earth pass, one jot or one tittle shall in no wise pass from the law, till all be fulfilled" (Matt. 5:17, 18).

Scholars often use "the law of parsimony" when they have to make a difficult decision. The law says that when explanations are otherwise equally adequate, the simpler should be chosen. Is not that the case here? One can use very complicated arguments and reasons to justify why the sanctity of the Sabbath shifted to Sunday. However, in the end it comes down to what makes the most sense and what is the most obvious answer. The answer is: God made the Sabbath day, and human beings for their own convenience have declared it to be changed to another day. Is not the old adage still true that declaring the world is flat does not necessarily make it so? As someone has said, "When plain sense makes good sense, seek no other sense."

The real issue here is that the Ten Commandments still say "Remember the sabbath day, to keep it holy" (Ex. 20:8). This, then, brings us back to our question: "Does it really matter what your opinion is or what you do?" The answer is a resounding yes! God cares what you think!

Perhaps the motive behind all that we think is summed up in the words of 1 John 3:22 — "because we keep his commandments, and do those things that are pleasing in his sight." If what we think and do is done simply and humbly to please God, then the following text will be an honest expression of our opinions and actions: "For this is the love of God, that we keep his commandments: and his commandments are not grievous" (1 John 5:3). And as we do so, we have solved one of modern religion's strangest mysteries.

The Mystery of the Unpardonable Sin

Unlike the way it is depicted in the cartoons, we don't really have a good angel on one shoulder and a bad one on the other to guide our decisions. Instead, every mentally stable person has a God-given conscience. The Latin root for the word *conscience* means a joint knowledge or a coknowledge. Our conscience is a system we have built into us that permits us to compare good and bad, right and wrong, safety or harm. However, there can be a problem with what goes into our conscience. As the computer adage states: "Garbage in, garbage out!" Or as Proverbs 23:7 states: "For as he thinketh in his heart, so is he." The apostle Paul told his young friend Timothy that people can have "their conscience seared with a hot iron" (1 Tim. 4:2), a statement that we would understand to mean scarred over or closed off. Such may be the case with the unpardonable sin.

Jesus said: "Wherefore I say unto you, All manner of sin and blasphemy shall be forgiven unto men: but the blasphemy against the Holy

Ghost shall not be forgiven" (Matt. 12:31).

A commentary on the life of Christ entitled *The Desire of Ages*, by Ellen G. White, states: "Whatever the sin, if the soul repents and believes, the guilt is washed away in the blood of Christ; but he who rejects the work of the Holy Spirit is placing himself where repentance and faith cannot come to him. It is by the Spirit that God works upon the heart; when men willfully reject the Spirit, and declare [Him] to be from Satan, they cut off the channel by which God can communicate with them. When the Spirit is finally rejected, there is no more that God can do for the soul. . . .

"It is not God that blinds the eyes of men or hardens their hearts. He sent them light to correct their errors, and to lead them in safe paths; it is by the rejection of this light that the eyes are blinded and the heart hardened. Often the process is gradual, and almost imperceptible. Light comes to the soul through God's Word, through His servants, or by the direct agency of His Spirit; but when one ray of light is disregarded, there is a partial benumbing of the spiritual perceptions, and the second revealing of light is less clearly discerned. So the darkness increases, until it is night in the soul" (p. 322).

Those persons deeply troubled that they have committed the unpardonable sin demonstrate by their worried conscience that they have *not* committed it! A person suffering with a guilty conscience can receive peace of mind by yielding to the transforming power of the Holy Spirit and making wrongs right with God and fellow human beings. Scripture promises: "If we confess our sins, he is faithful and just to forgive us our sins, and to cleanse us from all unrighteousness" (1 John 1:9).

Hotter Than Hell?

Today many people believe that the devil, sporting cowlike horns, armed with a pitchfork, and wearing a red jumpsuit, rules over a fiery place to punish evildoers. Some of the ideas Christians have about hell remind one of the ancient concepts of the underworld. For instance, the Greeks and Romans thought of Pluto, the "ruler of the underworld," as holding a two-pronged fork in his hand. On one end of the Sistine Chapel in the Vatican, a painting entitled the "Last Judgment," by Michelangelo, clearly depicts the influence of this Greek and Roman myth. The painting depicts a river and boatloads of sinners being ferried across into the hell of the underworld, a concept from the ancient Greek and Roman concepts of hell.

But hell as described in the Bible is hotter than anything the ancient pagans or their modern-day copycats have imagined. Malachi 4:1 states: "For, behold, the day cometh, that shall burn as an oven; and all the proud, yea, and all that do wickedly, shall be stubble: and the day that cometh shall burn them up, saith the Lord of hosts, that it shall leave them neither root nor branch." Obviously, something that has neither root nor branch ceases to exist.

Jesus used a similar example when He spoke of the wheat and the tares (weeds) in Matthew 13:40: "As therefore the tares are gathered and burned in the fire; so shall it be in the end of this world." Farther on in verse 42 He talks of casting the children of the evil one into a "furnace of fire." Such is the final fate of all unrepentant sinners.

In Luke 12:46-49 Jesus speaks of punishment for the unfaithful and the unknowing. He says some shall be beaten with many stripes, some with a few. Thus He makes the point that there will be a judgment and that punishment will be given according to what a person deserves. However, at the same time there is a time limit as to how long a person will be punished. The Holy Scriptures do not portray God as a cruel, heartless tyrant who keeps people conscious in torment for all eternity. Common sense tells us that even those tortured by Stalin and other tyrants would eventually call for an end to the suffering of even these evil people.

Ezekiel 33:11 tells us: "As I live, saith the Lord God, I have no pleasure in the death of the wicked; but that the wicked turn from his way and live: turn ye, turn ye from your evil ways; for why will ye die?" Jesus further stated in Luke 9:56: "For the Son of man is not come to destroy men's lives, but to save them."

The absurd idea that God and Satan teamed up to punish bad people is outrageous. Indeed, God will punish evil people in exact proportion to what they deserve, but He is fully capable of doing it without the devil's help! The idea of the devil with horns and a pitchfork is a rude fable designed to paint the God of the universe as being a cruel tyrant working in harmony with evil.

One Christian writer has beautifully stated what it will be like after God takes the horns off of the devil. "Sin and sinners are no more. The entire universe is clean. One pulse of harmony and gladness beats through the vast creation. From Him who created all flow life and light and gladness, throughout the realms of illimitable space. From the minutest atom to the greatest world, all things animate and inanimate, in their unshadowed beauty and perfect joy, declare that God is love" *(The Great Controversy,* p. 678).

God's judgment on the wicked will be hotter than hell, for it will destroy them forever. Both their suffering and that of the innocent will cease, and only love will reign forever.

In What Unusual Places
Did Early Christians Worship?

The method of worship in the early Christian church found its origin mostly in the services of the Jewish synagogue. To form a synagogue, only 10 men needed to come together and make a religious assembly. Even small towns had a synagogue or a place of prayer in a private home. Services in the synagogues included prayer, teaching, preaching, and Jewish rituals. It is said that in Jesus' day Jerusalem had some 400 synagogues to provide for the various Jewish sects and language groups living in the city.

After the founding of the Christian church, Christ's early disciples followed the example of Jesus and worshiped in the synagogue and Temple as long as they were tolerated.

However, Christians began to leave the synagogues. Up until the close of the second century, Christians held their meetings in private houses or deserted places. The oldest-known Christian house church still in existence is at Doura Europus on the upper Euphrates and dates to about A.D. 240. Justin Martyr (c. A.D. 100-165) is quoted as saying: "The Christians assemble wherever it is convenient, because their God is not, like the gods of the heathen, enclosed in space, but is invisibly present everywhere."

It wasn't until the middle of the third cen-

tury that Christians enjoyed 40 years of un-
abated growth. During this period church
growth mushroomed so much that the Christian
historian Eusebius of Caesarea (c. A.D. 265-
339) said that "more spacious places of devotion
became everywhere necessary." Rome is supposed to have had as many as 40 churches.
Following a short period of persecution, church
building flourished again under Constantine the
Great. As the church grew and prospered,
Eusebius told of a large ornate church built in
Tyre between A.D. 313 and A.D. 322 that had
a fountain in the center of the atrium for washing hands and feet before one could enter the
church. Truly the miraculous growth of the
Christian church would have astonished the
early believers who huddled in private homes
and hidden locations to worship.

For Further Study

Lampe, G.W.H, ed. "The Oldest Christian House Church."
    The Cambridge History of the Bible.
Schaff, Philip. *History of the Christian Church.* Vol. 1, pp. 455-
    460; vol. 2, p. 199.

The Mystery of the Mark of the Beast

For centuries people have puzzled over the
following passage in Revelation 13:16: "And he
causeth all, both small and great, rich and

poor, free and bond, to receive a mark in their right hand, or in their foreheads."

In the Greek language the word for mark is *charagma,* which means a stamp, mark, or impress. Many people envision that every government in the world will force the entire population of our planet to have a Social Security-type number tattooed into their foreheads with invisible ink. This number, they say, will be scanned with ultraviolet light for identification purposes.

The thought of people receiving a mark would not have been new to John the revelator. In Ezekiel 9:4 a being tells the prophet in vision, "Go through the midst of the city, through the midst of Jerusalem, and set a mark upon the foreheads of the men that sigh and that cry for all the abominations that be done in the midst thereof." In this case the divine messenger instructs Ezekiel to put an X upon their foreheads.

While this was all seen in vision, it is important to emphasize strongly the principle behind the instruction. The only persons receiving the mark were those who cared genuinely about the corruption they saw all around them. God characterized them as being so deeply upset that they were sighing and crying in sadness. Their characters set them apart—the mark was only an outward sign of what God saw in them inwardly. Those who had the mark were not to be destroyed.

John the revelator's vision reverses the marking. This time the mark is placed on those who are about to be destroyed. However, the principle is the same. Those who reflect the character of God will not need to worry about the mark.

Another reference to setting aside people appears in Revelation 7:3, where an angel commands, "Hurt not the earth, neither the sea, nor the trees, till we have sealed the servants of our God in their foreheads." Again the emphasis is upon those who are "the servants of God." Here, instead of a mark, God uses a seal. It reminds one of the ancient practice of placing sealing wax on an object or letter and impressing one's seal in the soft wax with a signet ring. The ancients would also impress a signet seal into the soft clay of a jar. It showed ownership.

Somehow the idea of all the governments of the world acting as the devil's agents to round up everyone on the planet and mark them seems to be a magnificent stretch of the imagination. However, this very idea strikes fear and terror into the hearts of many Christians. They worry that the devil is going to sneak up behind them and trick them into receiving the dreaded mark. But such fears ignore Jesus' promise: "And I give unto them eternal life; and they shall never perish, neither shall any man pluck them out of my hand" (John 10:28). And furthermore, Jude 24 speaks of Jesus being able to keep His people from falling.

One should never forget that Jesus' sacrifice for our sins enables everyone to be a citizen of heaven. It is only by Christ substituting

His goodness for our badness that we are saved. We can neither add anything to it nor take anything from it.

Is there a mark of the beast? Indeed there is! However, it is not based upon some literal stamp on the forehead or hand. It is much more subtle and makes more sense. It is a character that has resisted the transformation of the Holy Spirit.

Fascinating Facts About Easter Sunday

Easter is the oldest annual festival celebrated by the Christian church. Most Christians observe it on the first Sunday after the first full moon that follows the first day of spring in the Northern Hemisphere. The actual date of Christ's resurrection is unknown; therefore, the date of the celebration of Easter wanders between March 22 and April 25, according to the phases of the moon.

Many questions have arisen about the origin of Easter and its associated traditions. People wonder how such symbols as Easter bunnies, colored eggs, and hot-cross buns fit into the death by crucifixion, burial, and resurrection of Jesus Christ. The answer is simply this—they don't.

Another oddity about this holiday is the very use of the word *Easter* in the Bible. The phrase in Acts 12:4, "intending after Easter to bring him forth to the people," actually contains a mistranslation of the word for Passover. It is thought that some well-meaning scribe substituted the word *Easter* for Passover to make the text a little clearer. Of course, no matter how well-intentioned the scribe may have been, he had no right to alter the text.

The word *Easter* is believed to have come from the Anglo-Saxon Eostre, the goddess of spring. The ancients held a festival for her each year at the beginning of spring. As previously stated, the inclusion of this word in the English Bible was a mistake.

Much more information about Easter and related subjects can easily be found in encyclopedias in your local library under the topic "Easter."

For Further Study

Latourette, Kenneth. "Easter." *A History of Christianity.*
Schaff, Philip. "The Easter Cycle." *History of the Christian Church.*

Facts You Need to Know About Bible Study Tools

Most people who keep a few tools around the house have an adjustable wrench. It is one of those one-size-fits-all wrenches that do a lot of things pretty well. It works just fine as long as you don't expect it to perform like the more specialized tools. So too with Bible study tools. You can spend a few dollars for a book or two, or you can spend thousands and collect an extensive library. Either way, every serious Bible student needs at least a few tools to work his or her way through the nuts and bolts of understanding the Holy Scriptures. Described here are some of the tools that you can buy at your local Christian bookstore.

Minimum Tool Requirements

You must have a good Bible, preferably one with a reference column down the center of the page to help you find where a similar or related passage may be found elsewhere in the Scriptures.

A Concordance

This is a book that lists the principal words of the Bible according to where they are found. Check to see what version of the Bible your concordance is based upon. Obviously, a concordance for the King James Version is of little help if you have a Today's English Version. Also, one should note that there are both compact concordances and exhaustive ones. For instance, the exhaustive concordance is so complete that it lists every word used in the Bible, including, for example, every time the word *of* appears. The advantage of the smaller concordance is its handy size, but one should remember that for lack of space it has to leave many words out.

A Bible Dictionary

A Bible dictionary is necessary because it can provide the student with information about people, places, and events found in the Bible. Since its emphasis is only on matters relating to the Bible, the information is much more specialized and useful than a standard dictionary.

Bible dictionaries also come in many sizes and varieties. For instance, the standard scholarly dictionary might be five volumes of very fine print. The more advanced student will soon realize a need for a multivolume dictionary.

More Advanced Tools

A Bible Commentary

Bible commentaries are simply collections of comments on the various passages in the Bible. As small as one book or as large as 20 or 30 volumes, commentaries are written from a wide variety of points of view, including Jewish, Catholic, and Protestant. In addition, within the various communities of faith, commentaries can vary from very conservative to very liberal ways of looking at the Scriptures. The reader should be forewarned that some religious scholars do not believe the Bible to be inspired and simply see it as a collection of ancient literature.

For the Very Serious Scholar

For those interested in really digging

deeply into the mine of God's Word, there
seems to be no limit to what is available. You
will find Greek and Hebrew materials and
study guides to explore the Bible in its original languages. Parallel versions of the Bible
may contain as many as six translations of the
Bible side by side for comparison. Also available are books called surveys of the Old and
New Testaments and books of systematic
theology. And of course, there are the multitudes of computer-based Bible study helps
and reference materials on CD-ROM for the
computer-literate.

Does It Really Say That in the Bible?

Familiar Sayings Not Found in the Bible:

1. Cleanliness is next to godliness.
2. In God we trust.
3. Where there is a will, there is a way.
4. Practice what you preach.
5. God helps those who help themselves.
6. Let your conscience be your guide.
7. A word to the wise is sufficient.

Familiar Sayings Thought to Be in the Bible

1. "Money is the root of all evil." It actually says: "For the love of money is the root of
all evil" (1 Tim. 6:10).

2. "Do unto others as you would have

them do unto you." It actually says: "Therefore all things whatsoever ye would that men should do to you, do ye even so to them" (Matt. 7:12).

3. "Be moderate in all things." It actually says: "Let your moderation be known unto all men" (Phil. 4:5).

4. "I'm almost persuaded." It actually says: "Almost thou persuadest me to be a Christian" (Acts 26:28).

Familiar Sayings and Phrases
That Really Are Found in the Bible

1. A drop in a bucket (Isa. 40:15).
2. Good for nothing (Matt. 5:13).
3. The skin of my teeth (Job 19:20).
4. One among a thousand (Job 33:23).
5. The apple of his eye (Deut. 32:10).
6. What aileth thee? (2 Kings 6:28).
7. Fled for their life (2 Kings 7:7).
8. Beat to pieces (Isa. 3:15).
9. Woe is me! (Isa. 6:5).
10. Two are better than one (Eccl. 4:9).
11. Wrap it up (Micah 7:3).
12. Half dead (Luke 10:30).
13. See eye to eye (Isa. 52:8).
14. Am I my brother's keeper? (Gen. 4:9).
15. What is truth? (John 18:38).
16. Out of the mouth of babes (Ps. 8:2).

Little-known Facts About
How Ancient Writings Were Made

The ancient Hebrew holy writings used in the Temple during the time of Jesus would have been written on long scrolls made of papyrus or animal skin. To make a scroll of papyrus paper, papyrus plants as much as 15 feet high would be cut into page-length sections and the outer rind stripped off. The soft pith would be cut into strips and laid slightly overlapping on a hard surface. On top of them would be placed another layer going in the opposite direction. The two layers would be made into one by hammering and pressing them together. After drying, the sheet would be trimmed to size, smoothed with pumice stone, and polished. Finally the sheets were pasted together in lengths up to 35 feet and rolled up to await use. The finished product was white or off-white in color and was as durable as the best handmade paper produced centuries later.

Animal skins would be tanned, scraped smooth, trimmed, and sewn together into rolls of parchment.

The ink consisted of lamp-black or soot mixed with gum to help it to stick. The scribe used a reed pen.

When some 20 or more papyrus sheets were glued together, producing a scroll about 25 to 35 feet in length, it was called a biblion, often translated "book" (see Rev. 22:18). The longest example ever found is called the great Papyrus Harris, which is now in the British Museum. It is 143 feet long!

The First Codex

A codex is the book form as we know it today. It has separate pages held together on one side and with writing on both sides. The codex, or book, has its beginnings in the writing tablets used by the Greeks and Romans. They took thin rectangular boards, hollowed them out slightly, and filled the cavities with a thin layer of black wax. Then they wrote on the wax with a metal tool and erased by turning the tool around and smoothing out the wax. Up to 10 of these writing tablets were tied together with string, forming what we would call a notebook.

The Romans improved the codex, or notebook, by substituting parchment sheets for the wooden leaves and using carbon ink that could be easily washed off. The next step was to substitute papyrus paper for the animal skins. We do not know when this idea blossomed, but it happened during the earliest days of Christianity and could have happened as early as A.D. 70. Some feel that the inventor may have been a Christian. The word *codex* comes from the Latin *caudex*, which means "a log of wood."

It is interesting to note that the oldest piece of the New Testament we have is a scrap from John's Gospel, dated about A.D. 130, from a codex.

For Further Study
Lampe, G.W.H., ed. "The Early Christian Book Production." *The Cambridge History of the Bible.*

What Does the Bible Really Say About Heaven?

At one time I didn't want to go to heaven. That is, if heaven was what I thought it was going to be. Please let me explain. As a boy I remember attending church and singing the hymn "Mansion Over the Hilltop." Maybe you've sung it also. The words were: "I want a mansion, a harp, and a crown." The hymn goes on to say of that heavenly mansion, "I want a gold one that's silver-lined." Unfortunately, the concepts presented in the song didn't grab me. First, I didn't particularly like harp music. Second, I never wore a hat, so a crown sounded terribly uncomfortable. Third, I enjoyed living in Georgia—in the center of God's creation. Living in a house of gold that is silver-lined didn't sound all that appealing. Think about it. If you had hiked in the north Georgia mountains or sat on the beach over at Savannah and watched one of those spectacular orange sunrises over the Atlantic, wouldn't you find a metal mansion to be kind of a cold and impersonal place?

Why would anyone want to leave all of this to strum a harp on a cloud? I ask, "If heaven isn't better than this, why would anyone want to go there?" And then one day a friend helped me clear up what the Bible really says about where the redeemed of all ages will live. It turns out I had it all wrong. My friend had me open my Bible to a statement Jesus made. Matthew, a disciple of Jesus, wrote it down, and we can read it for ourselves in Matthew 5:5.

Where is the eternal home of the saved to be? Matthew says: "Blessed are the meek: for they shall inherit the earth." Who will inherit the earth? The followers of Jesus. The earth is our inheritance. The thought shocked me! Was my friend trying to tell me there was no heaven? "No," he said, "not at all. But it does mean that this planet will still be our home base." He continued, "After all, aren't we made of the elements of this earth? We are part and parcel of this planet. Why would we want to move off somewhere?" He reminded me that the Bible says God created humanity from the dust of the ground. Or as we would say today, God used the elements of this planet to form our bodies.

But I still wasn't satisfied with the idea that I could continue to live on this planet. "What about pollution?" I asked. "What about nuclear waste and poison gas and old ICBM's buried in the ground?" I wondered about things like junkyards and burned-out trailer homes. Human history has been mostly a grisly cycle of wars. So I asked myself, "Who would want to live forever on this planet with all of the relics of our bloody past?" Ships full of dead men and women litter the bottoms of our oceans. Huge landfills surround our towns and cities. You'll remember we used to call them city dumps. Furthermore, graveyards full of people who suffered and died from terrible diseases cover the earth. And what about the empty beer cans and plastic trash that clutter our land?

As I saw it, we could never be happy or safe with all of the moral and physical pollution that has contaminated our planet. Then my friend showed me in the Bible that there was good news. The earth will be cleaned up. Its surface will be melted down and recycled. What does the apostle Peter say will happen to our polluted planet? Second Peter 3:10 states: "But the day of the Lord will come as a thief in the night; in the which the heavens shall pass away with a great noise, and the elements shall melt with fervent heat, the earth also and the works that are therein shall be burned up."

It will be the biggest recycling project ever known—God's great environmental cleanup project. This will be like declaring the earth as a massive Superfund site. Of course, the difference between God's Environmental Protection Agency and the government's is that God will not run short on money or equipment. The Bible says that He will not only recycle the planet's entire surface, but also clean up the atmosphere.

Some 700 years before Christ, Isaiah the prophet spoke of a re-creation of our planet.

"For, behold, I create new heavens and a new earth: and the former shall not be remembered, nor come into mind" (Isa. 65:17). John, the writer of the book of Revelation, also witnessed the fate of our planet and recorded what he saw: "And I saw a new heaven and a new earth: for the first heaven and the first earth were passed away; and there was no more sea" (Rev. 21:1).

What will the new earth be like? God spoke of His plans for our planet in Revelation 21:5: "And he that sat upon the throne said, Behold, I make all things new." One of those new things will be a capital for our world. The new world capital will not be Washington, D.C., or Rome, or Atlanta! The city's name appears in verses 2, 3: "And I John saw the holy city, new Jerusalem, coming down from God out of heaven, prepared as a bride adorned for her husband. And I heard a great voice out of heaven saying, Behold, the tabernacle of God is with men, and he will dwell with them, and they shall be his people, and God himself shall be with them, and be their God."

Will we like it there? Verse 4 states: "And God shall wipe away all tears from their eyes; and there shall be no more death, neither sorrow, nor crying, neither shall there be any more pain: for the former things are passed away."

After learning what the Bible says about heaven, I changed my mind. I wanted to be in God's heaven. A Christian writer once wrote of heaven: "The redeemed shall know, even as also they are known. The loves and sympathies which God Himself has planted in the soul shall there find truest and sweetest exercise. The pure communion with holy beings, the harmonious social life with the blessed angels and with the faithful ones of all ages who have washed their robes and made them white in the blood of the Lamb, the sacred ties that bind together 'the whole family in heaven and earth' (Eph. 3:15) — these help to constitute the happiness of the redeemed" *(The Great Controversy,* p. 677).

What Was That in Roman Time?

During the lifetime of Jesus, people in Palestine had two methods of telling time: Roman and Jewish. The Jews divided the day into two parts of 12 hours each, extending from about 6:00 p.m. in the evening to about 6:00 a.m. in the morning, then from 6:00 a.m. to 6:00 p.m. This formed a night-day combination of 24 hours that began with sunset. However, they counted their hours from sunrise. For instance, in the parable Jesus gave in Matthew 20, He tells of a man going out to hire workers at the third, sixth, ninth, and eleventh hours. To us today these times would be 9:00 a.m., noon, 3:00 p.m., and 5:00 p.m. because we use the Roman mode, which reckons from midnight to noon and noon to midnight.

The Bible refers to both ways of marking time. However, in the New Testament only John followed the Roman mode of reckoning. The rest of the New Testament writers used the Jewish system. For example, employing Roman time, when John 19:14 says "it was about the sixth hour," he meant it was 6:00 a.m. However, when Luke uses the Jewish system in Acts 10:9, "about the sixth hour" meant it was noon.

To make matters more confusing, the Jews and the Romans divided the night into "watches." The Old Testament spoke of the early, middle, and late watches. However, in New Testament times the Jews adopted the Roman practice of labeling the watches as the evening, midnight, cockcrowing, and morning.

Furthermore, the idea of dividing the day into 24 hours, an hour into 60 minutes, and a minute into 60 seconds seems to trace back to the ancient Babylonian astrologers and astronomers.

The Mystery of the Lost Books of the Bible

The Bible mentions many books that scholars and archaeologists have never found and probably never will. Of course, many of these early books were not necessarily religious ones. Often they consisted of collections of facts consisting of census lists, names of landowners, administrative boundaries, military rolls, records of booty from war, and other necessary memorandums. The Bible writers made extracts of them. The books included in the Bible are different from ordinary writings, though. The books of the Bible focus on sacred history, or, as theologians sometimes call it, "salvation history." Scripture is an account of God working through His chosen people for humanity's salvation. The Bible excludes many more books than it includes. Peter suggests that God in His wisdom limited what should and should not be part of the Holy Scriptures. "For the prophecy came not in old time by the will of man: but holy men of God spake as they were moved by the Holy Ghost" (2 Peter 1:21). Furthermore, Paul says: "All scripture is given by inspiration of God, and is profitable for doctrine, for reproof, for correction, for instruction in righteousness" (2 Tim. 3:16).

The books that we know were excluded from the Holy Bible because Scripture mentions them are:

1. The book of the wars of the Lord — Numbers 21:14.

2. The book of the kings of Judah and Israel — 2 Chronicles 16:11.

3. The book of Nathan the prophet — 2 Chronicles 9:29.

4. The book of the chronicles of the kings of Israel — 1 Kings 14:19.

5. The book of Jasher — Joshua 10:13; 2 Samuel 1:18.

6. The book of Shemaiah the prophet and of Iddo the seer—2 Chronicles 12:15.

7. The epistle to the Laodiceans—Colossians 4:16.

8. An unknown epistle to the Corinthians—1 Corinthians 5:9.

Actually, we could say that there are no lost biblical books, since no crucial information has been lost. There are only books of information that God chose to exclude from the Bible. Are we therefore missing something important? As Ellen White has said concerning the value of the material we have in the Bible today: "The mine of truth is never exhausted. The more you search the Scriptures with humble hearts, the greater will be your interest, and the more you will feel like exclaiming with Paul: 'O the depth of the riches both of the wisdom and knowledge of God!'" *(Testimonies for the Church,* vol. 5, p. 266).

For Further Study

Ackroyd, Peter R., and Christopher F. Evans, eds. "Books in the Ancient World." *The Cambridge History of the Bible.*
Unger, Merrill. *Introductory Guide to the Old Testament.* P. 17.

Where 43 of the Bible's Most Interesting Things Are Found

The Old Testament

The Creation . . . . Genesis 1

The Crossing of the Red Sea . . . . . Exodus 14
The Suffering of Jesus Foretold . . . Isaiah 53
The Shepherd Psalm . . . . Psalm 23
The Ten Commandments . . . . Exodus 20
The Tower of Babel . . . . Genesis 11

The New Testament

The Birth of Jesus . . . . Luke 2
The Beatitudes . . . . Matthew 5:1-12
The Christian Commission . . Matthew 28:19, 20
The Crucifixion . . . . John 19
The Golden Rule . . . . Matthew 7:12
The Gospel Message . . . . John 3:16
The Final Judgment . . . . . Matthew 25:31-46;
                               Revelation 20
The Love Chapter . . . . 1 Corinthians 13
The Lord's Prayer . . . . Matthew 6
The Parable of the Good Samaritan . Luke 10
The Preview of Heaven . . . . . . Revelation 21;
                               Isaiah 35; 66
The Resurrection . . . . Matthew 28
The Sermon on the Mount . . Matthew 5, 6, 7
The Two Great Commandments . . . Matthew
                               22:34-40

Facts for Special Needs

When afraid . . . . Psalm 27
When courage is needed . . . . Psalm 91
When in trouble . . . . Psalm 46
When making hospital visits . Revelation 21:1-4
When patience is needed . . . . . . Isaiah 40:31
When wrong seems to be winning . . Psalm 37

Facts About Wisdom

Can two walk together?	Amos 3:3
Cast bread on waters	Ecclesiastes 11:1
Dead flies	Ecclesiastes 10:1
Feed enemy	Proverbs 25:21, 22
Good name is better	Ecclesiastes 7:1
Happy is he	Proverbs 16:20
Integrity is better	Proverbs 19:1
Merry heart a medicine	Proverbs 17:22
Not by bread alone	Deuteronomy 8:3
Seven things God hates	Proverbs 6:16-19
Soft answer	Proverbs 15:1
The good old days	Ecclesiastes 7:10
Time to every purpose	Ecclesiastes 3:1
What doth the Lord require?	Deuteronomy 10:12
Wine is a mocker	Proverbs 20:1
Worth of a virtuous woman	Proverbs 31:10
Conclusion of it all	Ecclesiastes 12:13, 14

What the Bible Has Meant in My Life

A Personal Note

Perhaps the best way to give you an idea of what might be important in the Bible for you is to tell you what I found in it for me.

When our children were small, we decided, for their own good, that it was time to get them into a church. We had no personal preference about which church—just about any one was fine with us. Basically we thought our kids needed an exposure to church because it was our duty as parents. Also, a friend at work had told me that church was a good place to meet the important people of our community in case I needed a job someday.

We visited churches in our neighborhood, but none seemed to appeal to us. We half-heartedly attended now and then, but were more interested in sending our kids off to church than we were in accompanying them. However, through the providence of the Lord, a husband and wife began to study the Bible with us in our home.

It all got started in an odd way. A friend of my wife's asked me to sit in on a Bible study being conducted in her home. Wary of it because she had heard that the people giving the studies were teaching strange things, she asked me to go check up on them.

However, at the time I was so ignorant that I thought "grace" in the Bible was a woman's name and that the book of Job was pronounced "job." Certainly I was the last person who would be able to argue the Bible with anyone. But I now feel that God was working behind the scenes. During the first study I attended, the man giving it asked, "Where did we come from and where are we going?" I didn't have a clue, but I wanted to know.

The next week he began to let the Scriptures themselves explain the long list of questions I had concerning this world and the fate of its people. I was so fascinated with what the Bible revealed that I invited the man and his wife to come to our home for weekly studies. It amazed me to learn of the ancient struggle between good and evil, of the conflict between Christ and Satan. What was going on in the world around me started to make sense. I began to understand that there was a way out of the sinful world I was so much a part of. In time I realized what Jesus had done for me, that He had already won the battle, and that all I had to do was to accept Him as my personal Saviour.

Our studies went on nearly every week for a year and a half, until my wife and I had a good solid introduction to the Word of God. However, we were still not church members — just frequent visitors. Then one evening the elderly man who had been our patient teacher for so long finally looked me square in the eye and recited this verse: "Now when they heard this, they were pricked in their heart, and said unto Peter and to the rest of the apostles, Men and brethren, what shall we do?" (Acts 2:37). Then he asked me, "What are you going to do?"

That night I decided to follow wherever Jesus would lead. Now, almost 30 years later, I can only respond in gratitude for how my life has changed for the better. Today I understand what it means to have real peace. I now realize where I came from, where I am going, and how to get along until I get there! So can you. It begins when the Lord impresses you to ask the questions that can be answered only in His Holy Word. Now is the time to begin your study. The Lord will bless you just as He did me. The Bible will become far more than just a collection of interesting information. It will transform your life. All you have to do is ask.

For additional copies of this book and other books exploring some of the topics in this book, phone **1-800-765-6955,** or you may contact the author at CompuServe **74532,1172**